Gaslight

Gaslight
Lantern Slides from
the Nineteenth Century

JOACHIM KALKA

Translated from the German by Isabel Fargo Cole

nyrb **New York Review Books** New York

This is a New York Review Book
published by The New York Review of Books
435 Hudson Street, New York, NY 10014
www.nyrb.com

Copyright © 2013, 2017 by Berenberg Verlag, Berlin
Translation copyright © 2017 by Isabel Fargo Cole
All rights reserved.

Library of Congress Cataloging-in-Publication Data
Names: Kalka, Joachim, author. | Cole, Isabel Fargo, 1973– translator.
Title: Gaslight : lantern slides from the nineteenth century / Joachim
　Kalka ; translated by Isabel Fargo Cole.
Other titles: Gaslicht. English.
Description: New York : New York Review Books, 2017. | Series: New
　York Review Books | Includes bibliographical references.
Identifiers: LCCN 2016054317 (print) | LCCN 2017000226 (ebook) |
　ISBN 9781681371184 (paperback) | ISBN 9781681371191 (epub)
Subjects: LCSH: Literature and society. | Civilization, Modern—19th
　century. | BISAC: HISTORY / Modern / 19th Century. | LITERARY
　COLLECTIONS / Essays. | HISTORY / Essays.
Classification: LCC PN51 .K337 2017 (print) | LCC PN51 (ebook) | DDC
　809/.034—dc23
LC record available at https://lccn.loc.gov/2016054317

ISBN 978-1-68137-118-4
Also available as an electronic book; ISBN 978-1-68137-119-1

Printed in the United States of America on acid-free paper

1 3 5 7 9 10 8 6 4 2

Contents

In the nineteenth century, Girtanner assures us, in the nineteenth century we'll be able to make gold; and the nineteenth century shall soon commence, that's no mere conjecture now, is it? With laudable confidence and an interesting sort of elation the worthy man says: "Every chemist, every artist shall make gold; pots and pans shall be of silver and gold."—Now all artists shall happily resolve to starve for the insignificant remainder of the eighteenth century....

—FRIEDRICH SCHLEGEL, "On Incomprehensibility," *Athenäum*, 1800

The writer of this preface has several times been accused in print of "sneering at the nineteenth century".... No one of any intelligence at all who remembers it, though it were only the golden glow and hush that fell upon the world in the few years that preceded the end of Queen Victoria's reign, could treat it so.

—OSBERT SITWELL, *Sober Truth*, 1930

THERESE: A person like that, you ought to take him and toss him right out of the nineteenth century. (Exit through the side door)

—JOHANN NESTROY, *Neither Laurel Tree nor Beggar's Staff*, 1833 (Act 1, Scene 10)

Preface

WE HAVE a certain custom in our dealings with history, strange but hard to shed—we assign decades and centuries a hazy face, a demeanor, we dress them in a certain costume, speaking of "the 1920s" and the "nineteenth century" as though they were individuals. For a decade such as the "1950s," especially given its striking product design, one could indeed construct a certain physiognomy, but many of these decimal-based labels remain persistently vacuous. The term "nineteenth century," on the other hand, seems unusually loaded.

What difference does it make that the nineteenth century, from our perspective, has just taken one step back in the long line of past *saecula*? It is no longer our predecessor century; it is, as it were, the past perfect of our present consciousness. Or is it the present perfect, after a century of being the imperfect? Our historical subconscious harbors a complex sequence of tenses. We're proud of our present, we want to be contemporary; in the United States you hear the youthfully snarky comment "That's *so* twentieth century." But doesn't it thrill us when the abyss of the past gapes? When a prodigious poem about the nineteenth century's close, beginning with the evocation of a silent, smoldering summer evening, empty train platforms, distant factory noise, and searing memories of the Franco-Prussian War and the Commune, builds to the lines:

And now, as once before, an image reemerged:
Sharp, bright as polished brass,
Far above all strife shone Jupiter.
And now as then: Jupiter stood on high,
Of all the stars the only to be seen,
And gazed on the eternal earthly fight,
That at this hour seemed so barbarous to me.
And overcome I murmured to myself
With faint lips: twentieth century.

They are from Detlev von Liliencron's "At a Train Station." Here the twentieth century, which for us has run its course, looms menacingly as a future that the nineteenth century uneasily anticipates. The twentieth century... *Twentieth Century* is a charming screwball comedy from 1934 with John Barrymore and Carole Lombard, set almost entirely on a moving train (called "The Twentieth Century") on which the actors of the Oberammergau Passion Play beg a big Broadway producer to book them, and a little old man (Etienne Girardot), smilingly mad, goes through the compartments discreetly affixing to everyone's back a sticker bearing the laconic words of all apocalyptic prophets: "The End is Near." We can't grasp the twentieth century, but doesn't the nineteenth paradoxically seem to draw closer? Vaguely we know that the twentieth century's monstrosities originated there, and there fermented the upheavals (Latin: the revolutions) that would destroy the world of old Europe.

In a novella first published in 1829, and set around the same time, ultimately to become the second stop in the long itinerary of the *Comédie Humaine* ("Le bal de Sceaux" in *Scènes de la vie privée*), Balzac has an old aristocrat quiz a young man on his lifestyle and remark: "I am fond of young people, and I like to see them happy. Their happiness reminds me of the good times of my youth, when adventures were not lacking, any more than duels. We were gay dogs then! Nowadays you think and worry over everything, as though there had never been a fifteenth and a sixteenth century." This is an astonishing leap, far back past the French Revolution and the eighteenth century, and the young man's reply hardly dispels our astonishment: "But, monsieur, are we not in the right? The sixteenth century only gave religious

liberty to Europe, and the nineteenth will give it political
lib——" Here the old, rigidly conservative officer interrupts
in amusement, but the reader is left to ponder the meaning
of this reference to long-past *saecula*. Is it the *ancien régime*'s
sense of security, recalling long, almost unchanging stretches
of time? No doubt it is, but for the reader, as for the inter-
locutor, it seems like a gentle accusation: one is on intimate
terms with so little of history's past.

Of course, any century under close scrutiny is bound to
reveal a bewildering wealth of phenomena that foils the
attempt to construct any real common denominator. (Put
casually and with smug irony: "Que de choses dans ce sacré
dix-neuvième siècle! C'est que, sacristi, il y en a pour tous
les goûts!"—"What can't you find in this blessed nineteenth
century! Good lord, there's something for every taste!"
—Edmond and Jules de Goncourt, *Manette Salomon*, 1867)
True enough, but looking back, our ingenuous historical
instinct sometimes does see *one* face. It may twist in shifting
grimaces, gaze in profound horror, or radiate a naive hope
that we now find incomprehensible. Yet perhaps this is the
crucial thing: back then, when progress still helped, dread
could always let itself relax back into foolish faith.

There is something opportunistic about this compilation
of essays: the author aimed to make a book out of various
older pieces, and in order to tie up this bouquet of appealing

themes plucked by the wayside, he picked a century's time line to serve as a ribbon. If this arbitrary approach makes readers pose the same question—"Does the nineteenth century exist?"—perhaps they will forgive him the artifice. For behind this question lies the more pressing one: Will it be possible to say, one day, that the twenty-first century existed?

"The True Unity Is Given by the Police"

The initial or luminous twilight curve vanishes or appears on the horizon when the sun has reached 8° below the horizon. This point in time is referred to as the end, or beginning, of civil twilight.
—*Meyers Handbuch über das Weltall* (Meyer's Handbook of the Universe), 1961

THERE IS a fascinating text by Friedrich Schiller that has remained almost entirely unknown: the abandoned dramatic fragment *Die Polizey* (The Police). The spelling—*Polizey* instead of the modern *Polizei*—adds a nice touch of period atmosphere, making the work seem, as indeed it is, both old-fashioned and intriguing. Schiller worked on the plan primarily from 1799 to 1801; crimes and intrigues were a favorite subject of his, and indeed his only novel *Der Geisterseher* (*The Ghost-Seer*, it too a fragment, though a much longer one) is set entirely in an atmosphere of crime and shadowy conspiracy. To begin, let us cite the description of a house search in the novel:

On removing the altar and some of the boards of the floor a spacious vault was discovered. It was high enough, for a man might sit upright in it with ease, and was separated from the cellar by a door and a narrow staircase. In this vault they found an electrical machine, a clock, and a little silver bell, which, as well as the electrical machine, was in communication with the altar and the crucifix that was fastened upon it. A hole had been made in the window-shutter opposite the chimney, which opened and shut with a slide. In this hole, as we learnt afterwards, was fixed a magic lantern, from which the figure of the ghost had been reflected on the opposite wall, over the chimney. From the garret and the cellar they brought several drums, to which large leaden bullets were fastened by strings; these had probably been used to imitate the roaring of thunder which we had heard.

On searching the Sicilian's clothes they found, in a case, different powders, genuine mercury in vials and boxes, phosphorus in a glass bottle, and a ring, which we immediately knew to be magnetic.... In his coat-pockets were found a rosary, a Jew's beard, a dagger, and a brace of pocket-pistols. "Let us see whether they are loaded," said one of the watch, and fired up the chimney.

"Jesus Maria!" cried a hollow voice, which we knew

to be that of the first apparition, and at the same instant a bleeding person came tumbling down the chimney.

Not only is all this highly entertaining, it reveals *The Ghost-Seer* as a sort of counter-model to *The Police*. Here Schiller describes a vast machinery of deception (encompassing the above-mentioned apparatus for simulating ghosts, with its magic lantern, electrical machine, and costume props), an agency of crime and confusion capable of engendering virtually impenetrable enigmas. By contrast, his main outline for the *Police* play begins as follows, cold and clear:

The action begins in the audience chamber of the Lieutenant of Police, who is questioning his officers and expatiating on all the branches of police activity and all the districts of the great capital. Thus the spectator is swiftly thrust into the midst of the vast city's workings and sees the great machine's gears in motion. Informers and spies from all classes … A vast amount of action must be handled, and it must be ensured that the spectator is not confused by the great variety of incidents and the number of characters. There must be a guiding thread that holds everything together… [the characters] must be connected to one another directly or through the surveillance of the police, and finally everything must resolve itself in the audience chamber of the Lieutenant of Police.—The true unity is given by the police, which provides the impetus and ultimately brings about the developments.

The vast city is Paris, which Schiller never visited, but knew from numerous books, especially Louis-Sébastien Mercier's great work *Tableau de Paris*. The vast city appears as a great machinery of gears, and confronting it we see the police as a control mechanism, a machine for the covert enforcement of order. While the *Ghost-Seer* sets up a theatrical apparatus of façades, humbug, confusion, and chicanery, the *Police*—this seems to be Schiller's great plan—takes over the whole conglomeration of equipment to serve as props for a power agency of rigorous enlightenment and order, the representative of a superior state.

We find a certain phenomenon in the output of dilettantes and dramatic geniuses alike: a lavishly profuse list of dramatis personae and extras, followed only by a few notes on plot twists, without any fully developed scenes (a classic, Rabelaisian example is Goethe's *Hanswursts Hochzeit*). In the case of Schiller's dramatic sketch, this profusion, spanning pages, is the very object of the author's interest; the concrete plot twists never get off the ground, and while the notes are evocative enough, in practice the actions pictured

9

might well have proved highly problematic to stage, with their details about poisons and strategically deployed ladders. These preliminary ideas, which cannot be explored here, amount to a miniature encyclopedia of the penny dreadful. The crucial thing is that the police are not merely an agency for preserving public order and hunting down miscreants, their task is not merely to keep track of the profusion, they are meant, and strive, for greater things. Schiller sees them as a sort of higher authority whose task, both particular and general, is to guarantee human happiness. For us this is an alien notion. Yet it is quite in keeping with the general drift of constitutional thought in the eighteenth and, to some extent, the early nineteenth centuries, when *Polizeiwissenschaft* (the science of policing) was responsible for reflecting on the proper order of the polity. While all the administrative and, later, investigative specialties would gain more and more weight, the fundamental idea of a police force is still the universality of the "proper order." In a great novel about the end of the nineteenth century we experience a concept of the police that was later lost; the author demonstrates it to us ironically. In Joseph Conrad's *The Secret Agent* (1907) a feeble-minded adolescent suffers vicariously whenever animals are beaten or people are treated unjustly. On a carriage ride he is shocked to see—or so it is explained to him—that the poor driver is forced to whip his poor horse to feed his poor children: "Bad world for poor people." But innocent Stevie comes up with a solution:

"Police," he suggested confidently.

"The police aren't for that," observed Mrs. Verloc cursorily, hurrying on her way.

Stevie's face lengthened considerably. He was thinking. The more intense his thinking, the slacker was the droop of his lower jaw.

And it was with an aspect of hopeless vacancy that he gave up his intellectual enterprise.

"Not for that?" he mumbled, resigned but surprised. "Not for that?" He had formed for himself an ideal conception of the metropolitan police as a sort of benevolent institution for the suppression of evil. The notion of benevolence especially was very closely associated with his sense of the power of the men in blue. He had liked all police constables tenderly, with a guileless trustfulness. And he was pained. He was irritated, too, by a suspicion of duplicity in the members of the force. For Stevie was frank and as open as the day himself. What did they mean by pretending then? Unlike his sister, who put her trust in face values, he wished to go to the bottom of the matter. He carried on his inquiry by means of an angry challenge.

"What are they for then, Winn? What are they for? Tell me."

Here Schiller's utopia of a "benign" surveillance power serving universal justice has become the dream of a feeble-minded boy—shaped by the profound perturbation of pity, but lacking all rationality.

Celui qui a le secret a tout.

—MOTTO of the Olivet family

Schiller's penchant for sensational subjects, for lurid tales of robbers, conspirators, and criminals, his attempt to carry on the tradition of Pitaval's French collection of *causes célèbres*—significantly, this is a fascination closely related to his interest in the biographies of great men, especially the ancient example of Plutarch's *Lives*. Both come together beautifully in *The Robbers*, when Karl Moor expresses the disgust with "this age of puny scribblers" that overcomes him when he reads of great men in Plutarch. Such frustrated souls seek out great individuals to study, on stage, their glamor, their limitations, and their entanglements. Schiller's great unfinished dramatic project, *Demetrius* (unfinished not because the author lost interest or reached the limits of his ability, as in the case of the *Police*, but because death intervened), attempts to outdo all that came before. Not just geographically, with Russia's endless, panoramic vastness—it presents a hero who is dubious from the very start, a false tsar, a pretender, though Schiller does insist that the hero must initially be convinced of the authenticity of his ambiguous role. But *The Police* would have shown something still more peculiar: the hero swallowed up by the institution. Schiller's first stroke of dramatic genius was entitled *The Robbers*, but ultimately it tells the story of a great individual, not a collective. The play could just as well be called *Karl Moor* or *The Robber*. With *The Police* such a thing would be impossible. Schiller's aim was to show the romantic appeal of a state apparatus. In this sense the fragment belongs to a strange and sparsely populated tradition: here we see the heroization of the administrative, the auratization of the driest thing imaginable. Of course, the charm arises from iniquity's picturesque proximity. The fascinating thing about Schiller's *Police* is that the whole mass of conspiratorial secrecy that in *The Ghost-Seer* is still on the dark side, the side of evil, has passed to the good apparatus of state order; it is as though the "Invisible Superiors" from a novel about secret societies were now governing the nation. It almost seems a bizarre anticipation of the romantic intertwinement of the police apparatus and the underworld that Balzac would soon so brilliantly demonstrate. In several of the novels of the *Comédie Humaine* (*Illusions Perdues, Père Goriot,* and *Splendeurs et Misères des Courtisanes*) Balzac deploys Vautrin, a great, superior criminal, as a sort of übermensch of the underworld, only to make him, in the end, the chief of police. *La dernière incarnation de Vautrin* (Vautrin's Last Incarnation) is the title of the final section of the *Splendeurs* in which this transformation takes place, as the suicide of Vautrin's protégé Lucien de Rubempré causes the great man's heart to break. (In switching sides, Vautrin reflects the biography of Vidocq, the flamboyant criminal, police informer, and, ultimately, police official with whom Balzac was closely acquainted.) In constructing a brilliantly ingenious police force, Schiller does not openly take the dubious detour through the criminal realm, but on an indirect level the two spheres have a constant tendency to overlap—his notes clearly reveal a delight in the "police spies' ceaseless changes of costume" and the "utmost extremes of mental states and morals."

In fact, Schiller's fragment is especially interesting when regarded in terms of a literary form that had not yet emerged at the time—that is, as a forerunner of the crime novel. On the whole, as we know, that genre tends to deify the detective and denigrate the police. At one point G. K. Chesterton has a policeman say to an amateur, mocking and resigned: "Ours is the only trade … in which the professional is always supposed to be wrong." The private detective who investigates a crime as part of his lonely profession, or by inclination and chance, sees more than do the ponderous police and is more morally reliable; when the detective belongs to the apparatus himself, he becomes a loner within it. Returning to Paris, Inspector Maigret feels old and inept around the increasingly young, intellectual, impertinent examining magistrates, and they treat him rudely. And so, to the fullest extent possible in a cycle of workplace novels, the policeman is transformed back into a romantic individualist within the apparatus.

Schiller's work marks a point at which the police could still be conceived as heroic and full of mystery. To the extent that current crime novels allow the police any heroism, it is the heroism of resignation, the obstinacy of the bureaucrat futilely committed to his duty. He can guarantee order no longer, only the stoic endurance of his own impotence. But even here there is a connection between Schiller's work and the crime novel: though social chaos is depicted, the passionate focus is on the precision of the ordering imagination. The crime novel, even and especially in its naive form, is a way of unifying disparate realities: "The true unity is the Police."

In this fragmentary police drama, Schiller left us a little meditation on the mystery of perfect order. Having begun his drama project with an extravagant profusion of secrets, as he experimented he may have begun to realize what Bertolt Brecht observed in his *Refugee Conversations*: "One could say that disorder is when nothing is in the right place. Order is when in the right place there is nothing." For all his prodigious store of riddles and costumes, perhaps Schiller discovered that the dramatic depiction of an apparatus of universal order tends to become stultifyingly dull.

It would be an illusory aim to read a work of literature, major or minor, for an unambiguous moral. But Schiller's *Police* fragment seems to hint at the extent to which the desire for comprehensive surveillance and control, even in the guise of promoting social good, originates as an aesthetic desire. As a playwright, Schiller places himself in the role of one who wishes to control a vast body of material—the imagined reality of a metropolis, which can stand as a cipher of an entire state. In turn, his aesthetic failure might point to a fundamental confusion in the mentality of order promulgated by the science of policing: its privileging of the *aesthetic*.

The connection between aesthetics and order is exemplified by a curious episode in the literature of German Classicism. The passage, famous but perhaps not famous enough, is found in Goethe's eyewitness account of the Siege of Mainz. He describes the events of 1793 that led to the end of the short-lived Jacobin republic in the Electorate of Mainz. Goethe, who was staying in Mainz as an envoy for his duke, witnessed the precipitous withdrawal of the French and the "Clubbists," i.e., the Francophile German Jacobins, from the city, and the crowd's increasingly threatening behavior, especially toward the latter. When one of the Clubbists was nearly lynched, Goethe hastened to intervene, saving his life by cajoling and threatening the crowd. Afterwards a friend, astonished and reproachful, asked him "how I cared to risk so much for an unknown and perhaps criminal person." Goethe resorted to the joking defense that he could not allow the square in front of his prince's house to be defiled by such an outbreak of violence, "and said, at last, rather impatiently: 'The fact is, it is part of my nature; I would rather commit an injustice than suffer disorder.'"

Here everything turns equivocal, and that is what makes the story so odd. We see Goethe excuse a heroic deed—whose foolishness he himself may have immediately regretted—by citing his need for order, and he explains his empathy with a harassed opponent as an indifference toward justice. This says a great deal about order, on a low or high level, and the implications of our desire for all things to unfold in an orderly fashion.

Schiller's flirtation with the notion of letting the police order the vast jumble of information about Paris that so fascinated him—Paris, it seems, was already the "capital of the nineteenth century"—and the hints as to how his concept of the police would aestheticize the notion of order and mechanize the notion of justice form a vignette in the history of our mentality of order. My little essay is merely a mosaic piece helping to construct what we might call a metaphysics of the police in the nineteenth century, a metaphysics that includes my last quote, from Kierkegaard: "As for myself, I am not what the times perhaps crave, a reformer, in no way; nor am I a profound speculative intellect, a seer, a prophet—no, I have, if you please, to a rare degree I have a definite detective talent."

If Only We Could Stop for a Moment, or: "Der World Iss Not Yet Ready for Mine Invention"

[M]y Iris kept working on a detective novel in two, three, four successive versions, in which the plot, the people, the setting, everything kept changing in bewildering bursts of frantic deletions—everything except the names (none of which I remember).... All the odd girl could ever visualize, with startling lucidity, was the crimson cover of the final, ideal paperback on which the villain's hairy fist would be shown pointing a pistol-shaped cigarette lighter at the reader—who was not supposed to guess until everybody in the book had died that it was, in fact, a pistol.

—Vladimir Nabokov, *Look at the Harlequins!*

Anything can be turned into a weapon—a handful of sand knotted in a stocking can bludgeon a person, and a wisp of air, as a bubble in a hypodermic needle, kills the patient without arousing suspicion; that we know from mystery novels. Nothing is too trivial to become a deadly riddle; generations of readers have learned that a tiny bit of water can kill a person without leaving a trace—if you put an icicle in a thermos flask and take it into the Turkish baths (Edgar Jepson and Robert Eustace, "The Tea Leaf"). That is the hallmark of our private, artisanal infatuation with death. Nothing is too trivial. And so the detective in mystery novels is classically seen huddled over barely perceptible details, and the forensic pathologist, the detective's most powerful current incarnation, searches for tiny perforations and microscopic lesions. At the opposite end of the spectrum is a criminal, indeed military force with a virtually infinite reach: nothing is too big for a murderous plan. The extent to which trashy films merge with military strategy is seen in the way *Star Wars* has colored our language. The military sphere, more than any other, is governed by breathless innovation that seizes on *every* detail: an endless sequence of inventions. The historical inability to stop for a moment and ask whether a new invention is actually necessary most easily finds its alibi in the military: everything that is possible must be developed, otherwise we'll be defenseless (because it *is* possible).

This inability to ignore novelties goes hand in hand with the fear of failing to grasp the significance of a crucial technological advance. It inspires stories that reflect the fairy-tale trope of scornfully rejecting a magical object out of ignorance. One classic anecdote is related by Baron Hermann von Eckardtstein (*Lebenserinnerungen und politische Denkwürdigkeiten*, 1919). According to the author, Bismarck once spoke of himself as lacking any feel for technology whatsoever; to bolster his—possibly correct—view that in a statesman this could not be seen as a shortcoming, he claimed that Friedrich II and Napoleon had lacked this feel as well. And then Bismarck gave the following example: Once, at Johannisburg Palace, Prince Metternich had told him how he was called to Napoleon, then residing in Vienna's Hofburg, shortly after the Battle of Austerlitz in 1805. "Suddenly, he said, the door of Napoleon's study opened, a young man virtually came flying out, and Napoleon hurled the coarsest curses after him.—Then he told Metternich in a tone of utter indignation that Livingston, the American ambassador in Paris, had dared to send a madman with a letter of recommendation to him in Vienna. This idiot had claimed to have an invention that would allow him, the Emperor, to land troops in England independent of the winds and tides—with the aid of boiling water."

That, then, was the legendary meeting of Napoleon I and Robert Fulton, inventor of the steamship. (The anecdote beautifully conveys how absurd the key feature of a technical innovation can sound when articulated: the invasion of England is supposed to be pulled off "with the help of boiling

water.") There are some realistic details in the little story—
Livingston did invest in the development of steam naviga-
tion. But it is clearly a fabrication, not least because Fulton
would have been no stranger to Napoleon. Several years
before, he had offered France a different ground-breaking
invention, also claiming that it could decide the struggle
with England: a submarine.

Fulton, a distinguished engineer from Pennsylvania who
initially earned the money to pursue his technical projects
as a miniature portraitist, had come to France in 1797 after
encountering various setbacks in England. The antagonism
between Great Britain and post-revolutionary France, whose
heroes included the victorious General Bonaparte, was coming to a head; the full extent of the French public's obsessive
invasion fantasies is illustrated by articles in the *Vossische
Zeitung* (no. 149, 1797): "The [Parisian] citizen Thilorier
desires to stage an attack on England not only with airships,
but also with divers. If, he quite rightly notes in his announcement, my first project has been regarded as absurd, this one
will be judged still more harshly: It is possible, without great
danger or expense, to march an army in battle array, with its
horses, stores, artillery, and baggage, from England to France,
and, if circumstances require, have an invisible fleet rise
momentarily from the bottom of the sea to take the army
back to France. He begs the public not to judge hastily, and

promises further enlightenment in 14 days."—And in no. 153: "Several days ago the announcement was made in Thilorier's name that at a certain time he planned to take a stroll on the bottom of the Seine. Many curious onlookers gathered, but Thilorier did not appear. Some even claim that his airship and diver project is meant as a satire on the impending expedition against England.—Meanwhile, the famous [balloonist] Blanchard offers to equip hot-air balloons to burn the enemy's stores and occupy his forts." That is the context; the whole decade teems with pamphlets, articles, and cartoons revolving around a French invasion of England—with *Montgolfières*, or through a tunnel under the Channel. And these are the years in which Fulton offered the French government plans for a submarine which he called the "Nautilus." It was supposed to navigate secretly under the hulls of English battleships and plant mines for subsequent detonation. After Fulton had built the *Nautilus* at his own expense and tested it in the Seine, he was permitted to mount a trial attack, but the new boat proved too slow for the British ships. After (typically for him) switching sides, the inventor had a similar experience in England, this time hunting French navy units.

As is customary with these sorts of offers, Fulton offered the assurance that this terrifying new weapon would—precisely because of its terrifying nature—usher in an age of peace. His futuristic technology served the cause of improving the world. The dialectic of weapons that will ensure peace if only they are terrible enough is not exactly foreign to us. Indeed, it held its own for fifty years, a fact that occasionally allows us to forget the madness of its underlying logic.

FRIEND: *Well, how was the inventors' fair?*

TRAVNICEK: *Don't even ask!*

FRIEND: *Why, what's the matter?*

TRAVNICEK: *I invented something too. But they didn't take it.*

FRIEND: *What did you invent, Travnicek?*

TRAVNICEK: *The ship's propeller.*

FRIEND: *But that's already been invented.*

TRAVNICEK: *I didn't know that. Such an Austrian fate.*

FRIEND: *And is that what you're annoyed about?*

TRAVNICEK: *I'm not annoyed about that, I'm annoyed that the others did know.*

—HELMUT QUALTINGER, "Travnicek and the Vienna Fair"

Many of the letters, pleas, offers, and notifications that passed between Fulton and the French and British governments over the years have been preserved. Among other things, they show France's distracted interest in the *bâteau poisson*, an interest that did, at any rate, ultimately prompt First Consul Bonaparte to appoint an assessment panel including such prominent authorities as Laplace, Volney, and Monge. In practice, the boat proved slow and unreliable, and the end came in 1801 when Napoleon impatiently rejected what seemed a purely eccentric project. (And Fulton was a truly eccentric pursuer of projects, someone who in 1797 produced a treatise presenting his two chief obsessions—a system of inland canals and his submarine boat—as symmetrical techniques of salvation: *a Universal betterment of Humanity, through a constructive system of Canals, and a destructive system of Torpedoes.* This is the origin of the word "torpedo" in the sense that we are familiar with. There is an uncanny aspect to one of his improvised money-making projects: around 1800 he erected a large panorama in Paris depicting *L'incendie de Moscou.* There were no doubt participants in Napoleon's Russian campaign who recalled this prophetic spectacle as they witnessed Moscow's great fire in 1812.)

Remarkably, in many older histories—and even in the current edition of the Encyclopædia Britannica ("The French government rejected the idea, however, as an atrocious and dishonourable way to fight")—one reads that moral outrage alone held back Fulton's contemporaries from adopting his weapon. Napoleon, in particular, appears here as a man who rejects Fulton's plan in disgust.

One should keep in mind that few people in world history—and surely none in the long nineteenth century—have been as heavily mythologized as Napoleon. We might need to go back to Alexander to find an equivalent. Part of Napoleon's myth is definitely a certain scorn of technology—the modern technology that goes beyond the workmanlike knowledge proper to a lieutenant of the artillery. Both as a politician and as a commander he privileged the will instead. This will was presumed to be so strong that for a long time people could not quite believe in the emperor's death. There is always a popular tendency to believe that great or notorious men are not actually dead; with no other modern figure did this rumor persist as stubbornly as with Napoleon. A vast proliferation of pamphlets blossomed solely around the fiction that he went on to serve the sultan as a Turkish commander—having converted to Islam?—and was responsible for defeating the Russian troops in 1828. In a fabulous reversal of this pious longing for mortality's suspension, the wag J. B. Pérès, a librarian in Agen, published an ingenious satire on Dupuis's mythography *Origine des cultes*, in which Christ is the sun and his apostles are the signs of the zodiac. Pérès's pamphlet, from 1835, purported to prove that Napoleon had never existed: that he represented a solar myth, with his four brothers as the seasons, his twelve marshals as the signs of the zodiac, and his legendary Russian campaign as the sun's path in winter.

Napoleon seems to be a magnet for legends. And to the last his legend was most peculiarly intertwined with the submarine boat. In the year 1834 newspapers reported that a notorious adventurer by the name of Johnstone had tried to sell a submarine, this time to the pasha of Egypt; this craft, too, was supposedly able to cause devastating damage by planting explosives on the hulls of enemy ships. "Johnstone avers that in this way he could destroy an entire fleet in fourteen days," reported the Hanover newspaper *Posaune*, and went on: "We know that during Napoleon's lifetime he conceived the plan of using his submarine to spirit the man of the century away from St. Helena.... But what are plans, what are projects! Johnstone lives on with his invention, and Napoleon died on St. Helena."

What is behind the fantastic anecdote of the great Napoleon's indignant rejection of the submarine? It reflects the principle—once dominant in Chinese historiography—that history ought not to record what occurred, but rather convey what the proper story should have been. Perhaps the curious legend of Napoleon's contempt for the submarine reflects a retrospective dread of one of the uncanniest of weapons. Certainly it perpetuates the hope that there could be such a thing as a sovereign who disgustedly rejects certain technological possibilities.

Why, Hal, 'tis my vocation, Hal; 'tis no sin for a man to labour in his vocation.

—FALSTAFF in *Henry IV*, Part 1, Act 1, Scene 2

In the anecdote, the great Napoleon—by virtue of the "demonic" superiority which Goethe saw in him?—scornfully dismisses the submarine; it violates the standard of military honor. But in fact one of the privileges of the great individual is that of flouting all accepted boundaries. A submarine called *Nautilus*—haven't we heard that somewhere? Yes, it is the name, surely an implicit reference to Fulton, of the submarine that spreads death and destruction in Jules Verne's novel *Twenty Thousand Leagues under the Sea*. This ship is the apotheosis of the cozy bourgeois salon with its library, grand piano, and panorama windows overlooking the ocean floor— and it is the headquarters of destruction. Its captain's name is Nemo. (His name recalls the ruse of Odysseus, who introduces himself to the Cyclops as "Oudeis," or Nobody, so that when he finally blinds the Cyclops, the giant's friends, hearing his cries that "Nobody" has harmed him, turn away, unwilling to help.) But Nemo is not a man hounded by divine wrath and the vicissitudes of fate, he is the inexorable master of his world, the Romantic übermensch as scientist. Like others of Verne's protagonists, such as "Robur le Conquérant," he pits himself against mankind. While Frankenstein, the Gothic novel's other great inventor, constructs his artificial man out of a Faustian urge to create and fantasizes about a universal world order—it is no coincidence that he studied in Ingolstadt, the center of the Illuminati conspiracy—Nemo is and remains an adept of destruction. He is a forebear of the mad scientists whose shrill laughter echoes through the B-movies. Occasionally, as in Nemo's case, their delight in destruction is seen as having a tragic cause, as vengeance for some great injustice. But in keeping with the narcissistic logic of these fantasies, this injustice may be something purely banal, a personal slight.

This is beautifully depicted by the great comics artist Jacques Tardi, second to none in his loving evocation of the Belle Époque with its archaic yet uncannily menacing technical apparatuses, that realm between the museum and the industrial laboratory. With images recalling a film by Georges Méliès, with the rhetoric of the maniacally eccentric mad scientists of the Grand Guignol, his classic *Le démon des glaces* (1974) takes us inside a titanic Arctic iceberg at the center of a zone of inexplicable ship disasters. The young hero wakes up there after the sinking of his ship; standing in front of him is his uncle, presumed dead, who had long been occupied with strange experiments. Now he and his colleague, two classic *savants fous*, strike up the litany of the aggrieved outsider: "At the university, we were young and naive and still labored under the puerile notion of working for the good of humanity. But as the years passed and we suffered identical humiliations, we realized that it was fruitless for men of our mettle to try to improve the lives of those idiots, indifferent as they were to our discoveries and ever eager to drag us through the mud." Stories of this kind are miniature melodramas of wounded narcissism, and in passing they say a good deal—almost everything—about our lust for armament.

And she has been down in the depths of the sea.
—IBSEN, *The Wild Duck*

Whether plying the turbulent seas of childhood fantasy, as in Woody Allen's *Radio Days* and Gahan Wilson's exquisite comic strip *Nuts*, or setting out to war as *Das Boot*, the military submarine is a German legend, a triumph of World War I. There is a growing awareness that the greatest memorial to all the shades of this war's lunacy, including the complacency of daily routine, was created by Karl Kraus in his epic drama *The Last Days of Mankind*, written "to be performed on Mars." But the precision with which Karl Kraus analyzed the preconditions of this lunacy has not been broadly recognized. Exploring Wilhelminism under the heading "The Techno-Romantic Adventure," he shows that we are no longer able to grasp our own technical capabilities. Their implications outstrip our moral imagination, and we take refuge in romantic phrases—in an age of poison gas and flamethrowers, Wilhelm II liked to speak of "sharply honed swords." One of the key scenes in Kraus's vision unexpectedly ushers in Leonardo da Vinci. Amidst the endless-seeming procession of "apparitions," like Shakespearean phantoms, that concludes Scene 55 of Act 5 of *The Last Days of Mankind*, we behold an "old-fashioned workshop," and Leonardo is heard: "—and I shall not write down the why and wherefore of how I manage to stay under water for as long as I can; and I will not publish or explain it, because of the malign nature of man, who would only use it to commit murder on the ocean bed by breaking the hulls of ships and sinking them, with all the people aboard—"

This dramatic quote leaves out the conclusion of Leonardo's remarks. In the original, they end: "Nevertheless I will impart [other methods], which are not dangerous because the mouth of the tube through which you breathe is above the water, supported on air sacks or cork." In other words, Leonardo restricts himself to conveying strategies in which the attacker remains vulnerable even under water, as his *bocca di canna* reveals him to his target. Leonardo da Vinci was a man who (in a famous letter to Lodovico il Moro of Milan) tossed out a single sentence describing himself as a painter, while commending himself at length and in detail as an architect and engineer for civilian and especially military projects of all kinds—what made this inventor of cannons, forts, scythed chariots, machine guns, and battering rams hold back, filled with reluctance and revulsion, when it came to setting down notes for a submarine? We do not know. One might suppose it is just another example of his mantra "I shall not write . . . ," intended to protect himself from imitators and competitors. But "by reason of the malign nature of men" makes his reasoning apparent.

It is difficult to gauge Leonardo's motivations for writing these words. In any case, for Kraus, looking back, his stance became a towering example of necessary renunciation. The significance of this passage from *The Last Days of Mankind* lies in its contrast with the barbaric smugness of the patriotic zeal for the German submarine war ("We blow them up and sink them soundly, but sensitively too!"). In Act 5, Leonardo is immediately preceded by the twelve hundred horses

Count Dohna drowned, and immediately followed by sing-ing children's corpses "on a piece of flotsam," two of the twelve hundred victims of the *Lusitania*, a passenger ship famously sunk by a German submarine. When the Basque government issued an information brochure in May 1937 on the bombing of Guernica—which Franco's regime and the Nazis tried to pass off as arson committed by fleeing Basque troops—it couched the historical truth of the Ger-man air raid in words citing two World War I atrocities: "We know who the murderers were—it was the ones who sank the *Lusitania* and burned the University of Leuven."

Both horses and children are the victims of an explicitly technological force that flies in the face of nature. By selec-tively quoting Leonardo, Kraus salutes a stance that has been lost, or perhaps was only supposed to have existed—the ability to reject a technological advance despite its feasibility. For Kraus, this appears as mankind's final chance for survival in its last days.

A good deed is easy to do, but it is hard to decide whether it is called for.

—LEONID LEONOV, *Notes of a Small-Town Man*

One of Billy Wilder's lesser-known films, *The Private Life of Sherlock Holmes*, features perhaps the most charming appearance of a figure who has come to epitomize old-fashioned narrow-mindedness, though there is clearly much more to her than that: Queen Victoria. The film plays with Holmes's haughty romantic inexperience (already emphasized by Conan Doyle) by having a woman lead the master detective astray—a lady whose Belgian-French name conceals the German spy "Ilse von Hofmannsthal." The plot turns on the disclosure of a project by the British intelligence service: they are testing a submarine manned by midgets and disguised as the Loch Ness Monster. The climax comes when the new weapon is finally presented to the Queen, played by Molly Maureen. She reacts with undisguised horror and disgust. This sort of weapon is "unsportsmanlike, it is un-English, and it is in very poor taste." (Perhaps we are hearing, in a different national costume, a distant echo of the Napoleon anecdotes.) She goes on: "Sometimes we despair of the state of the world. What will scientists think of next?" The context is ironic; the final question, as such, is not.

The Queen's attitude in Wilder's film, the British crown's brusque rejection of such a weapon, permanently conflates the historic and the mythopoetic, seeming covertly linked to her most famous historically documented utterance. Everyone knows the words; they were recorded late (in the memoirs of Lady Caroline Holland, 1919) and without reference to a specific situation, but stand as a sort of epitaph which the era chiseled for itself: "We are not amused." I believe we need to hear these words anew. If anything can save us, it might be the constant meditative repetition of this mantra, with an additional version for technological contexts: "We are not interested." This might help us to grasp that our automatic interest in the next technological stage of destruction or amusement is the common denominator of our annihilation (by amusement, by destruction).

Truth thrives in the margins. In closing, let us take a look at an American comic book published in 1942—though, crucially for this context, based on daily comics from November 30, 1936, to April 3, 1937. This Disney comic, by Floyd Gottfredson and others, is called *Mickey Mouse and his Sky Adventure*, and is still written very much in the spirit of the nineteenth century. An adventure in the sky, it begins with Mickey and his bumbling, indispensable companion Goofy flying along in a two-seater airplane (somehow they seem to be connected to a military base). An automobile flies past, and an elderly gentleman greets them amiably. It turns out that this Doctor Einmug has discovered "some new kind of power with a tremendous force"; he is already being pursued by foreign spies. One of them—a familiar figure, Black Pete—tries to steal the revolutionary formula, but Mickey manages to foil the attempt. But though Colonel Doberman has entrusted him with the hysterically urgent mission of finding out this information ("We must get it before someone else does!"), the scholar refuses to share his knowledge.

Doctor Einmug is a kindly scientist of almost magically advanced intelligence. Remarkably enough for 1942, the year after Pearl Harbor, and even in 1936 reflecting a generous infatuation with tradition, he is identifiably a *German* scientist in the venerable old-school manner. At a time when American comics were deploying all their superheroes against the Nazis, here—anachronistically, nostalgically— we see a roly-poly little bearded scholar with a white lab coat, pince-nez, a top hat (or a black, Biedermeier-era cap), and a long-stemmed pipe who speaks with a thick Teutonic accent. His name is a pun on "Einstein"—already a legend, as this indicates. Because the "stein" can mean a beer tankard, it is replaced by "mug," a slang word for "face." This unlikely and unprepossessing hero proclaims the reason why no one can be allowed to possess his knowledge: "I am sure you will understand why you can neffer haff mine formula! Der world iss not yet ready for mine invention! It would bring only sorrow...und fighting...und killing!" Dismayed, Mickey asks: "But, Doctor Einmug! What are you gonna do with your formula?" "Don't worry, mine friend! Nobody else will get it! You will neffer hear of it again...or me either!" And a few minutes later Dr. Einmug escapes to another planet, along with his laboratory island that floats amidst the clouds. Mickey and Colonel Doberman philosophize bemusedly that they'll never be able to talk about this adventure: no one would believe them. "All we can do is just shake hands on it...and *forget* the whole thing!"

Perhaps forgetting is just the art we need to learn; it would parallel the masterfully abrupt disappearance of the fugitive scientist. Harald Weinrich's great study *Lethe: The Art and Critique of Forgetting* ends with a reflection on the "oblivionism" of science—the scholar's sense of powerlessness when faced with masses of material that mount ever higher and ever more rapidly. Might we hope for a sequel that would write the epistemology of active *forgetting*, the sober and rational refusal to know, the renunciation of a possibility?

Last Chance Saloon
Reflections on Balzac's
A Woman of Thirty

"You know I'm going to be twenty-five in June?"—"You are?"—"That's a quarter of a century. Makes a girl think."—"About what?"—"About the future. You know—like a husband?"

—MARILYN MONROE and TONY CURTIS in the sleeping-car washroom of the Florida Limited, in Billy Wilder's *Some Like It Hot*

WE HAVE COME to understand that the stages of life (like so many things) are social constructs, that seemingly immutable things like age, death, childhood, and love are subject to the strangest metamorphoses and fashions. Without negating their reality, this variability clothes it in bewildering costumes. One of life's topoi—which are variable, yet constant in their significance—is the sense of *now or never*, the notion of a point in the unfolding of the years when a thing becomes urgent, when it is already almost too late. In *Some Like It Hot* the subject is touched on casually, briskly, yet quite decisively in the conversation between Sugar/Marilyn Monroe and her new girlfriend (the man in drag she'll fall in love with). The *like* in "You know—like a husband" does not denote the choosing of some example; rather, it is something like an equal sign—a future would *be* a husband. Wilder's comedy promptly sabotages the notion of a husband as synonymous with the future; Sugar Kowalczyk ends up back in unmarried bliss with one of those flaky saxophone players she'd resolved to avoid, and at the end of the movie only Jerry/Jack Lemmon is faced with the problem of getting dragged to the altar by Mr. Osgood/Joe E. Brown. All the same, Sugar's words are worth reflecting on. The film was made in 1959 and set in 1929; in either year Monroe's categorical "That's a quarter of a century. Makes a girl think" would sound utterly plausible. Twenty-five years on this planet? High time to think about the future! About marriage. The need to end up with a man, that is, the plan for snagging a husband, is ramped up to an improbable and hence comic level when presented as the dogged hunt for a millionaire. And yet this is serious: a woman's age is coded according to her matrimonial potential.

There is something fascinating about the shifting perception and self-perception of age, with astonishing examples everywhere. Let us open Saint-Simon's inexhaustible *Memoirs*: "I had been that morning to wait on Madame,

39

who could not refrain from saying, in a sharp and angry voice, that I was doubtless very glad of the promise of so many balls—that this was natural at my age; but that, for her part, she was old, and wished they were well over." Madame utters the words "for her part, she was old" in the carnival season of 1692. She is the second wife of Monsieur (the honorary title of the king's brother in *ancien régime* France) Philippe, Duc d'Orleans, the brother of Louis XIV; she was born as Elisabeth-Charlotte of Bavaria and lived from 1652 to 1722. This is a forty-year-old speaking—one tiny detail among thousands. Another, famous vignette of the staging of age is presented in the title of a novel that draws a sharp caesura in a woman's life.

In Balzac's vast novelistic oeuvre, a marvelously mad mixture of system and anarchy, some of the titles, at least in the context of his huge taxonomic endeavor, suggest a quasi-sociological approach or ambition: *The Peasants, Poor Relations, The Country Doctor, The Celibates, The Lesser Bourgeoisie.* Others use proper names: *Eugenie Grandet, Ursule Mirouët, Madame de la Chanterie, La Duchesse de Langeais.* For most readers, *La Femme de trente ans (A Woman of Thirty)*, one of the best-known titles in the *Comédie Humaine,* probably floats in an odd suspension between concept and individual name. So what kind of a woman is she? Leaving out all the colorful detail and—though this is next to impossible—the melodrama, the novel tells the following story: A young woman marries a good-looking and utterly mediocre man; disappointed in this marriage, she becomes profoundly depressed. A doctor heals her; they fall in love; we see the desperate lovers, unable to bring themselves to consummate the act of adultery, in a moment of crisis, a crucial heart-to-heart in the heroine's boudoir. The encounter is interrupted by the husband's unexpected arrival: to avoid compromising the lady, the lover flees onto the windowsill, where he is forced to spend the entire freezing night, and later dies of the effects. The lonely woman suffers terribly. Now thirty, she finally finds a lover (Charles de Vandenesse, brother of Félix de Vandenesse, one of the ubiquitous recurring characters who link the narratives of the *Comédie*); her husband tacitly accepts the relationship. Their legitimate daughter drowns the cosseted younger son, product of the adulterous relationship, in a fit of jealousy. Later this guilt-ridden girl flees her parental home with a mysterious murderer; her father finds her years later, now married to the outcast, on board a corsair ship, surrounded by children and treasures—one of those melodramatic flourishes that not even Balzac can pull off without making the reader grin incredulously. Another daughter conceived in adultery unwittingly falls in love with her half-brother, and when her mother tries to dissuade her from this incestuous relationship, she is met with the fatal words: "Mamma, I thought you were only jealous of *the father*—" The mother dies of what can only be described as a broken heart.

This is the terrain, ploughed up by the finger of God and the lightning bolts of "fate," on which something resembling a social type is to be depicted.

Who, for instance, painted the old and the beautiful of the Empire better than he?

—SAINTE-BEUVE

The old and the beautiful! But the beautiful age as well, and this, in some way, is meant to be the true theme of *A Woman of Thirty*. Yet there are many contradictions between its tangled plot and its succinct title. The genesis of the tale (written between 1830 and 1842) is a philological puzzle. Increasingly ambitious, the author aimed to rework a whole series of early publications, very disparate stories, in the context of a completely new plan. The material that Balzac so laboriously melded together to produce the quasi-novel *A Woman of Thirty* was originally meant to have a framing narrative—the individual stories were supposed to remain autonomous, embedded almost unaltered in a background story. The concept changed as Balzac decided to experiment with the principle of recurring characters that would make his great novelistic oeuvre so unique, structuring the reworked text, without the distancing effect of a frame, as part of a virtually unbounded portrait of society. The eschewal of the popular Romantic principle of the framing narrative is meant to bring the work closer to "reality"; however, the author had to struggle with the unreality of his old inventions. Six older stories published in various newspapers became the novel's six chapters: "Early Mistakes," "A Hidden Grief," "At Thirty Years," "The Finger of God," "Two Meetings," and "The Old Age of a Guilty Mother." Balzac laboriously pieced together these heterogeneous stories; again and again his letters report things such as: "I have been into the country for six days to finish something in a hurry." (July 30, 1834) He is "exhausted by the fatigues of conception" (or creation—*de la conception*). The novel shows the traces of this patchwork method, and shamelessly trails melodramatic odds and ends—inventions on the level of Balzac's earliest period. Part of the truth about this work is that Gide once asked whether Balzac had ever written anything worse.

Balzac comments on the novel himself in his letters to his lover and confidante Madame Hanska, occasionally to comical effect. On the second chapter, "Soffrances inconnues," he writes: "It is a horrible cry, without brilliancy of style, without pretensions to drama. There are too many thoughts in it, and too much drama to show on the outside. It is enough to make you shudder, and it is all true. Never have I been so stirred by any work." (August 26, 1834) "We are reprinting at this moment the fourth volume of the 'Scènes de la Vie privée,' in which I have made great changes in relation to the general meaning in 'Même Histoire';" as the novel was called at that stage, "so that Hélène's flight with the murderer is rendered almost plausible. It took me a long time to make these last knots." (January 1, 1836)

Almost plausible—*presque vraisemblable*. Here an author who owes many of his finest effects to melodrama reveals how strongly he feels obliged to dress the outré in the garb of "probability." For by this point his intention is to dissect social issues—but still using his old instruments. Only one of the novel's chapters includes "À trente ans" in its title—the middle chapter, describing a fulfillment soon to be destroyed, with capricious inexorability, by "the finger of God." It was Sainte-Beuve who noted that Balzac had developed the "theory of the woman of thirty years . . . with all her merits, her advantages, and her ultimate perfections." But this theory has something gothic about it; the woman is diagnosed by the flickering Bengal light of melodrama.

Since the Marquis de Sade's death in Bicêtre Hospital, adultery, debauchery, and other, unspeakable vices have found no one to describe them more brazenly and understandingly....

—LOUIS VEUILLOT, "D'un manifeste littéraire" (1840)

Balzac was long regarded as the epitome of the risqué writer—due less to the artificial medieval ribaldry of his Rabelaisian *Contes drôlatiques* than to the scandalous nature of all the contemporary adultery motifs in the panorama of the *Comédie*. Nowadays adultery has lost its luster, a banality noted with a shrug of the shoulders, at most evoking vague embarrassment or gentle sympathy. It no longer possesses the glamor of sin. Flaubert, in *November*, was still able to describe the fascination of that "indecent" word: "Henceforth, there was one word that seemed to me the most beautiful of all human words: the word *adultery*. An exquisite enchantment hovers hazily over it...." This fascination surely stems in part from the "beautiful"—sonorous, exotic, dignified—French word *adultère*, which expresses the magic of transgression with a suggestive, Latinate gravity lacking in the dry, crude German word *Ehebruch*. But semantics aside, at that time—by dint of law, theology, and public morals—the *act* was still able to have an existential aspect. Or put differently: the dissolute aristocratic casualness of eighteenth-century sin no longer prevailed absolutely. With the Restoration, marriage had regained a certain solemnity, and that was what made adultery so fascinating.

As late as 1888 a distant echo of this fascination resounded through the French press, in one of those tragicomic cases where life seems determined to imitate art (the classic example being all the suicides provoked by reading *Werther*). A law student shot his lover and tried to kill himself, then defended himself in court by citing the corrupting influence of works of literature such as Alfred de Vigny's *Les Amants* and *La femme de trente ans*—specifically the scene in which the first, noble lover confesses to his beloved that he can no longer bear the impossibility of possessing her, and in fact had already formed the plan to shoot them both. (Inspired by this case, Paul Bourget wrote a famous "psychological" novel of its day, *The Disciple*, in 1889.) This is the glamor not of "sin," but of the heroic transgression of boundaries. Marriage is the boundary, and it is one whose dangerous violation is worthwhile.

"Passion daily gathers strength from the dismaying prospect of the coming days." This is one of the key statements in the novel that are intended to make the individual Julie d'Aiglemont into the social type of a woman of thirty. Many twists of the *Comédie's* labyrinth evoke the extreme manifestation of this "dismaying prospect": the "old maid." Even as a wife, as a lover, the woman of thirty is an old maid in larval form, filled with fear of a sexless life. This is what charges her with such passion—a passion that gathers "for the last time," seeking release on the threshold of resignation. This passion is the product of life's brevity, the social brevity of the female erotic life which must be contrasted with the fact that the men in the *Comédie*—unless earmarked for roles as eccentrics—do not age perceptibly over the decades.

To grasp this fear of aging, we need insight into the marital context. The title of the first—and only?—film version of the novel (by Edward H. Griffith, 1921) is both touching and comic in its naive, primer-like didacticism: *If Women Only Knew*. But there is something very real behind it. If women only knew *what*? ... How deceitful men are? It can't be meant in such a general sense. No, it must mean: If women only knew what marriage signifies! And this thought brings us close to the secret of Balzac's woman of thirty. Adultery has its sinister glamor only because marriage, in its insolubility, is filled with such profound tristesse. This insolubility is a nightmare. (Thus the aptness of Goya's depiction in no. 75 of *Los Caprichos*: "¿No hay quien nos desate?" A man and a woman are chained together, guarded by a gigantic, spectral owl that claws at them: "Can't anyone untie us?") The entire type of the "woman of thirty" is set against the background of this nightmare. Here we see how closely

Balzac intertwines what is given by nature and what is imposed on individuals by society.

... mes études sans fin ...

—BALZAC, writing to Madame Hanska

Within the grand scheme of the *Comédie Humaine, A Woman of Thirty* falls into the subsection of the "Scènes de la Vie privée." The first chapter of this sketch of private life begins, however, with a grandiose public spectacle, a description of the *grande armée*'s last parade at the Place du Carrousel before setting out into battle. A huge crowd is waiting for Napoleon; the two people we encounter at the beginning, a father and his daughter, are able to find a good spot only with the help of a young officer. Seeing the pretty, eager young Mademoiselle de Chatillonest (later Madame d'Aiglemont) in the crowd, the Emperor leans toward Duroc and says something to which we are not privy that makes the Marshal smile. A nice touch—the eagerness and beauty that bring smiles to the great men's faces ultimately bring ruin to the young woman who will marry the officer. This is one of Napoleon's six cameo appearances in the *Comédie*.

This figure, this titanic extra, is lit only obliquely, as when Laurence de Cinq-Cygne makes her petition on the eve of the Battle of Jena (*Une ténébreuse affaire*). But the great name echoes everywhere—even in the proud chatter of César Birotteau, who is named a Knight of the Legion of Honor, "possibly... by fighting for the Bourbons upon the steps of Saint-Roch on the 13th Vendémiaire."

The juncture between public and private—secretly expressed, as we will soon see, in the very figure of Napoleon—is the institution that preoccupied Balzac more than any other: marriage. One of his best-known titles is *Splendeurs et misères des courtisanes*; the majority of the narratives in the *Comédie* could implicitly be subsumed under the heading "The Splendors and Miseries of Matrimony." After all, the entire endeavor begins with an essay about marriage; the first piece that Balzac incorporated into his project, the initial nucleus of the *Comédie*, was a little tract from 1828 entitled *La Physiologie du Mariage*. And Napoleon provided him with dictums such as "Marriage is not an institution of nature" and "Laws are made to suit manners, and manners vary," statements that Balzac cites so as to weave his reflections on marriage around them.

This most industrious of authors produced prodigious amounts of writing, but fell far short of his still more prodigious plans. Of the twenty-eight planned "Scènes de la vie militaire" we have only two. Balzac's ambition, which was that his labyrinth of novels should set forth an encyclo-pedia of institutions, characters, and types, unfolding, in narrative fashion, a *complete* catalogue of representative social figures before the reader, failed brilliantly—to name just one reason, he died too soon. (Of great interest are the pieces of the *Comédie Humaine* which he noted down as titles or sketches but never managed to write—in the *Scènes de la vie privée* this includes *Les enfants, Un pensionnat de demoiselles,* and *Gendres et belles-mères.*) And the vast major-ity of the "Études analytiques" that were to crown the edifice of the *Comédie* went unwritten; the most substantial piece that has come down to us is the above-mentioned work on the physiology of marriage, which preceded the *Comédie* but in places already reveals its fragmentary outline. Char-acteristically, once embedded in this gigantic construct it was summarily retitled *Petites misères de la vie conjugale.* Physiology reveals marriage's (little) miseries.

The term "physiology" has a peculiar ring to it; it can firstly be explained as a fashion of the time. That age, intox-icated by the emerging potential of the natural sciences, was fascinated by the idea of turning social observation into a science; however, the sociology it developed continued to draw on romantic impressions. The favored title for express-ing this contradiction is "physiology." "There was once a happy time—it seems as though it were yesterday, yet it is already far remote—when two or three 'Physiologies' appeared each week. Hundreds were written each year. They were light pamphlets, prettily designed, charming, often quite witty and amusing, with no claim to transcendence, and always copiously illustrated by those gifted and malicious vignettists of the 1840 generation" as the "neo-icono-bibliomaniac" Octave Uzanne wrote half a century later in *La Nouvelle Bibliopolis* (1897). He describes this fad for literary physiology as "a light, subtle, ironically distanced art that can hardly be defined with precision and that, without excessive strain or exaggeration, possesses all the agility of the essences it seeks to describe." Uzanne constantly uses the adjective *léger* to emphasize the "lightness" and infor-mality of the literature of physiology. Recalling the first major work in that form, one readily concurs—Brillat-Savarin's *Physiologie du Goût* (1826) had a strong influence on Balzac's tract from 1828. Brillat-Savarin's work on taste (in food and drink) is still read by gourmets with a certain sense of reverence, and rightly so; it is buoyant, civilized, and urbane. By contrast, Balzac's piece has a brazen, boastful masculinity, the rather lumbering jocularity of winking col-lusion. This "physiology" soon reveals itself, quite openly and unashamedly, as a defensive manual for husbands: for long stretches it is couched as a guideline for preventing female deceit. All the same, one need merely turn the strategy of this traditional misogynistic humor on its head to diagnose marriage as a highly unsatisfactory institution for wives. The title *A Woman of Thirty* seems overly fraught with the claim to "representativeness" until one considers that the novel, behind the flames of melodrama, really does have an analytical theme: women and marriage. The year thirty, dictated seemingly by biology alone—and of course by the flukes of the decimal system—emerges entirely from this context.

The characteristic feature of these "physiologies" is the analysis of an "organism," an analysis that is allegedly precise and seemingly inspired by scientific models, yet executed in a highly subjective manner. They quickly take on an openly sardonic tone. As early as 1837 Flaubert wrote a similar piece, "A Lecture on Natural History—Genus: *Clerk*," beginning his description with the words "From Aristotle to Cuvier, from Pliny to Blainville, natural science has made great strides," then moving on to the question "Comment classer cet animal?" and deriving, from various details of clothing and body, clues that seem to point to different segments of the animal world. Here the form becomes pure satire. Balzac is still toying with a scientific claim—i.e. the claim to present an illuminating analytical description—that even his humor does not entirely negate. But when we regard physiology as a literary form, what vividly emerges is its capricious nature—paralleled later on by the supposedly exact but actually arbitrary definition of a type such as the "woman of thirty."

It is the opinion of many of Balzac's admirers, and it was the general verdict of his day, that in all this the greatest triumphs are the characters of women. Every French critic tells us that his immense success came to him through women—that they constituted his first, his last, his fondest public.

—HENRY JAMES, "Honoré de Balzac" (1875)

Balzac is one of the discoverers of the big city, and hence of quick-paced time. Time passes. A bill will be presented tomorrow, not a week from now; that is a primal situation in Balzac. To stave off suicide, old Grandet's brother would have needed money at a certain moment; the rich old man let the moment pass. Observations of this kind (melding, in a manner typical of the author, the sensational and the utterly mundane) imply a feel for the tempo of life—individual life with its days and years. The two great principles that organize Balzac's world are will and chance. Chance

53

would be another story, but when we speak of will in Balzac, we are speaking of his male characters.

The male will is capable of great and terrible things. (While Balzac's heroes have a penchant for writing big books, it is unusual that two of them, Louis Lambert and Raphaël de Valentin, should both write books on the will— *Traité de la volonté* and *Théorie de la volonté* respectively.) Balzac is perfectly capable of irony; the famous excessively extravagant gesture with which Rastignac, from the heights of Pére-Lachaise, issues Paris's flickering lights the challenge "Henceforth there is war between us" is followed by the malicious comment: "And by way of throwing down the glove to Society, Rastignac went to dine with Mme. de Nucingen." Yet again and again he naively celebrates the will as an omnipotent Romantic force, meant, in the spirit of Romantic physics, to represent something like a measurable energy. This will unites the most disparate characters of the *Comédie*, making the schemer Vautrin (masterful, flouting prohibitions, stopping at nothing) into the brother of such an utterly conformist, comically foolish figure as the perfume dealer César Birotteau, who, after his bankruptcy, works to rehabilitate his mercantile honor with virtually superhuman tenacity—drudgery that brings him success, but also a heroic death.

The more "feminine" Balzac's protagonists are, the more

likely they are to be brought down by a lack of will (like
Lucien de Rubempré). The will that achieves so much for
Balzac's men is less helpful to the women, for they have a
different connection to time, the time line of their lives. In
this sense the "thirty years" are like a wall which women's
energy cannot surmount. Adultery can breach it.

In a famous letter to Margaret Harkness from April 1888,
Friedrich Engels praises Balzac almost exorbitantly as an
author from whom he "learned more than from all the pro-
fessed historians, economists, and statisticians of the period
together." He writes of the Legitimist Balzac's description
of society: "He describes how the last remnants of this, to
him, model society gradually succumbed before the intru-
sion of the vulgar moneyed upstart, or were corrupted by
him; how the grand dame whose conjugal infidelities were
but a mode of asserting herself in perfect accordance with
the way she had been disposed of in marriage, gave way to
the bourgeoisie, who horned her husband for cash or cash-
mere..." Here Engels plays the worldly cynic a bit too vehemently. Reading Balzac, one sees how often this author sees
love, even (especially?) illegitimate love, as pure passion;
incidentally, even taking the cynical point of view it should
be noted that Balzac's adulterous wives are far more likely
to shower their lovers with presents than to let themselves
be presented with "cashmeres." But love is the most important

thing—"The Infinite, sensibly transmitted to us by the measureless sensual delight which may be experienced by God's creatures." That—as Balzac construes it—is what, in vanishing, ought to perturb the woman of thirty.

The interesting thing about Balzac's novel is how vividly it reflects a reality of the time: the horror of approaching an age threshold whose touch, with the inevitability of second nature, deprives a woman of love (thus implacably nailing the married woman to her marriage). And the degree to which, at the same time, the arbitrary nature of this arrangement, the capriciousness of the "physiological" pseudoanalysis, becomes visible. At the sore spot of this arbitrary arrangement, the great passion stirs, refusing to accept the boundary; here is the focus of a lucid insight into the monstrosity of marriage, which predicates the monstrosity of adultery—and the apparatus of melodrama must still be set into motion to turn an idea into a story. Even if the result is a peculiar one, here the question of the potential of a stage of life, its boundedness or boundlessness, is raised with the casual brilliance of a strategic title. Readers who care to trace this development further can follow it to a new level with Baudelaire's sublime poem "Les petites vieilles," where, a little while later, the poet and the decrepit old women meet under the banner of passion.

Goethe Was Not a Good German
Remembering Wolfgang Menzel

But I might see young Cupid's fiery shaft
Quench'd by the chaste beams of the watery moon.
—*A Midsummer Night's Dream*

IF ANYONE remembers Wolfgang Menzel today, it is probably as the epitome of the "denouncer" in Heinrich Heine's work, and as "Menzel, the Scourge of the French" in Ludwig Börne's delightfully titled essay. This preserves him in vague recollection as the antagonist of what was known as "Young Germany," but then most people aren't quite sure what that was either. At any rate, literary history still recalls Menzel mainly as a major opponent of that Young Germany. With this in mind, there is a certain appeal in beginning with quite a generous characterization of Menzel by a leading literary figure from that very group. It was published by Heinrich Laube in the *Zeitschrift für die elegante Welt* in

57

March 1834, just before the rift, the huge scandal that would land Laube himself in jail. Before citing this portrait, written by a man who was setting out to become Menzel's implacable opponent, some background is needed. Menzel's name is associated mainly with one journal, established in Tübingen and later relocated to Stuttgart. Johann Friedrich Cotta founded the *Morgenblatt für gebildete Stände* in 1807; in 1809 the journal gained a supplement entitled "Übersicht der neuesten Literatur" (Overview of Recent Literature), which began to appear more and more frequently, retitled "Literaturblatt" (Literary Pages) in 1819. The following year it became an autonomous publication, a separate journal of literary criticism—a detachment process comparable to the emergence of the *Times Literary Supplement* from the *London Times*. For the first five years, this independent publication was edited by Adolf Müllner—a man known chiefly as the author of *Schicksalsdramen* (Tragedies of Fate), a then-flourishing genre parodied by August von Platen in *Die verhängnisvolle Gabel* (The Fateful Fork). Müllner had written a melodrama of fratricide, *Die Schuld* (Guilt, 1813), that was incredibly successful at the time.

Now let us return to Laube: "For many years, thanks to the assiduous endeavors of the Cotta publishing house, the *Morgenblatt* has stood as a most admirable hub of German journalism. At a time when Germany appreciated the power of journals still less than it does today...the deceased Privy Counselor Müllner held the *Morgenblatt*'s literary pages in a stranglehold of something like blood lust. His grip was that of caprice, not of principles. Müllner was a one-sided, intolerant, brutal man who disguised his utter lack of poetic feeling with skilled rhetoric, spoiled by the fluke success of his abysmal *Guilt*, and dealt barbarically with anything that failed to arouse his meager sympathies.... There was a general sigh of relief when he died, fuming, in Weißenfels in Saxony. It was the death of the Marat of German literature. —Toward the end he had already grown impotent in his pugnacity, and his faction, Germany's so-called 'reviewers,' lost their power—those 'reviewers' who like brazen village dogs leap at the legs of hastening passersby and tear their trousers without ever looking these wayfarers in the face or in the eye, who merely gnaw, tug, chew on details without structuring and creating terrain. Their yapping faded away."

Now Laube describes the rise of Müllner's successor, Wolfgang Menzel, who succeeded to power, as one is tempted to put it, in 1825. "He brought Müllner's boldness and other, nobler aims to the critic's chair"—no armchair, but the *sella curulis*, the judge's bench—"and can be compared with those Greek heroes who with death-dealing hands descended on the land's monsters and malignant beasts, tearing out the forest's rotten old trunks and opening the land to the air and the sun. He made our literature arable, chased out drivel with mockery, gave the signal to smash the idols—with force and skill he joined battle against the authorities. In Germany, mind you, that is an important, historic achievement, for the authorities are our affliction, the authorities are the false gods in whose fetters we languish. Not long ago the boldest explorations stopped short if they came up against the very first letters of a name like Goethe or Klopstock, and a prominent professor was more sacred than ever was a Brahman in Delhi. We were ecstatic as the Indian fakirs if only we could crawl up in the sand and kiss his shoe. Our literary respect was even greater than our political respect. . . ."

All things considered, though a faint irony stirs, and will shortly come through more strongly, this is high praise: Menzel has liberated the attitude of the critic. A crucial key to the sympathy expressed here can be seen in the hostile, derisive mention of Goethe. "Wolfgang Menzel," Laube continues, ". . . thrust literature into the marketplace of life, forcing it to mingle with people. He tossed the rotten old scraps from the lecture halls onto the public squares so all the world could see that the worms had been at them; often, like a general amidst gun smoke, we have seen him swathed in the academic dust he raised from that old rubbish. Wolfgang Menzel's merit is that of a hero who has raised a land up from its primitive state.—But a land does not remain primitive forever, and heroes are required only for a time; had Perseus, with his club and Medusa's head, mounted the Acropolis of Athens in Pericles's day, it would have been a strange sight to see. Constant heroism tears out even the healthy, necessary trees...."

Menzel, Laube goes on to say, does not judge haphazardly, like Müllner; he has categories, but that has become a problem in itself. "Instead of Müllner's haphazardness, he came with ready-made, closed categories; he became the Hegel of our critics.... He passes judgment according to these categories, and a vigorous patriotism dictates his words, animating and inspiring them, whether he is speaking of drama or geography. But courage is the crucial word, everything must be filled with courage, must perform gymnastics, display heroic strength, even the lover as he kneels before his maid. If his beloved spurns him, he must lay about him with a vengeance...." In the censure and above all in the praise conveyed by this witty portrait one should keep in mind Laube's strategic interests; all the same, it is a fine appreciation of Menzel and shows the high esteem in which his early work was held.

Let us take a brief look at Menzel's biography. He was born in 1798 in Waldenburg, Silesia, as the son of a doctor. "Everything must perform gymnastics": as an adolescent he actually did join the patriotic gymnastics movement, founded by Friedrich Ludwig Jahn, which played such a crucial role for the youth of that time, especially in Prussia and the northern and central German states; Menzel's first publication, at the age of twenty, was the pamphlet "The Veritably True Story of the Hard Struggles and Final Victory of the Good Cause of Gymnastics at a School in the City of Breslau." He studied history and philosophy in Jena; when August von Kotzebue was assassinated by the student Karl Sand and the authorities cracked down on the nationalist movement at the universities, Menzel, who belonged to a nationalist fraternity, was expelled. He continued his studies at the University of Bonn, but was forced out once again due to his "demagogic activities." In 1820 he went to Aarau, Switzerland. His first publishing endeavor, a collaboration with Friedrich List and Alexander Follen, among others, was the journal *Europäische Blätter*, which appeared in Zürich from 1824–1825; it was here that he first documented his aversion to Goethe. In 1824 he returned to Germany, choosing Heidelberg so that he could conduct research in its library. Finally, in 1825 he was invited to Stuttgart to take over Cotta's *Literaturblatt*, which he edited until 1849; after Cotta ceased publishing the journal, Menzel carried on with a publication of his own (also simply called *Literaturblatt*) and as an independent writer. In Stuttgart, a year after taking the position that secured his long-term livelihood, he married a pastor's daughter, Johanna Christiane Bilfinger, who died soon after him and is buried at his side; the couple had nine children. Menzel gained significant influence with monumental works such as *Die deutsche Literatur* (German Literature, two volumes, 1828) and *Geschichte der deutschen Dichtung* (History of German Poetry, three volumes, 1875), as well as writing a *Geschichte Europas* (History of Europe) and a plethora of works with titles such as *Eine Kritik des modernen Zeitbewußtseyns* (A Critique of Modern Self-Consciousness), *Die Naturkunde im christlichen Geist aufgefaßt* (Natural History as Conceived in the Christian Spirit), and *Elsaß und Lothringen sind und bleiben unser* (Alsace and Lorraine Are and Shall Remain Ours). His own literary efforts, such as *Rübezahl. Ein dramatisches Märchen* (Rübezahl: A Fairy-Tale Drama) and *Furore. Geschichte eines Mönchs und einer Nonne aus dem dreißigjährigen Kriege* (Furor: The Tale of a Monk and a Nun in the Thirty Years' War), are slight, though it must be said that they were not considerably worse than most upmarket popular fiction of the day. Until his death on April 23, 1873—that is, for nearly half a century—he never left Stuttgart apart from two brief journeys, to Austria in 1831 and to Italy in 1835. Following his turbulent student years, his life remained outwardly uneventful. The obituary that appeared in the *Allgemeine*

Zeitung presents a picture evoking some of this eternal sameness: "Menzel's external appearance can truly be called imposing. Beholding the stately man—broad shoulders crowned by a head with hair rippling down to his nape, dressed in a simple grey coat, a sturdy rattan cane in his left hand and a bundle of books under his right arm—as he stepped out of his cozy little house set in an orchard near the old city wall in one of Stuttgart's little-frequented streets"—Hospitalstrasse—"and strode about town with a firm tread, one had to say that this man was quite cut out to instill a certain awe and catch the eye of all who met him. . . ." The outward uneventfulness of this daily walk was the foil to a tempestuous literary life.

Let us pause for a moment to study the proclamation which Menzel issued in 1829, several years after taking up his post as Cotta's man at the *Literaturblatt*, at the point when it began to appear under his own name. This substantial text, which begins with the words "In the years to come, the undersigned will edit the *Literaturblatt* according to a new plan," concludes by stating that in the case of sophisticated works, as opposed to purely fashionable and popular literature, "I shall . . . always rate the poetic spirit higher than the poetic form, and hold to the principle that the most beautiful form cannot excuse base or ignoble contents. Hence I shall take a resolute stand against the faction that has deluged Germany with a flood of verses beautifully constructed but devoid of spirit, and from which has issued an overestimation—unworthy of the nation and the spirit of our age—of works that conceal an unworthy sense beneath a charming form. Secondly, I shall rate the human spirit that must animate true poetry... higher than the spirit of individual schools that take the character of one time, one people, one poet as the criterion of the beautiful, lapsing into the idolatries known as the Greco-, Indo-, Anglo-, Shakespearo-, Goetho- and other manias."

This passage is an example of extremely dubious rhetoric. In the context of Menzel's critical practice, "rating the poetic spirit higher than the poetic form" means the vilification of Goethe's late poetry. And here the "humane spirit" of "true poetry" is pitted against Goethe, against Shakespeare, against classical aesthetics (Grecomania) as well as the Romanticism of the Schlegel brothers (Indomania). Menzel did extol some great authors—Novalis, Jakob Böhme, Annette Droste-Hülshoff—but upon closer inspection even his warmest appraisal is the product of ideology. He is constantly doing precisely what he claims to reject on principle: he praises a school of thought or what he sees as belonging to one. He seems to have esteemed Christian Dietrich Grabbe mainly for his anti-Napoleonic plays, while Jean Paul serves as Goethe's antithesis. Menzel's praise has been forgotten; none of his panegyrics, unlike Börne's eulogy for Jean Paul or Georg Herwegh's "Ein Verschollener" ("A Lost Man") on Hölderlin, still move us today; only his hate-filled censure continues its shadowy existence as a classic case study, as one might almost say in the sense of a pathology of criticism.

Half a century after the manifesto cited above came the rift that caused Heine to brand him a denouncer and that to this day, not undeservedly, has made him a *bête noire* of literary history. With his review of a novel by Karl Gutzkow and an ensuing series of articles, Menzel precipitated a ban on writings from the "Young Germany" group that affected Gutzkow, Laube, Ludolf Wienbarg, Theodor Mundt, and Heine. This sequence of events, the biggest literary scandal of the Metternich period, displays Menzel as the henchman of reactionary governments that operated through imprisonment and censorship, as the man who denounced an entire generation of German literature to the reactionaries.

In 1841, reviewing Gutzkow's book on the deceased Börne, Herwegh offered a memorable characterization of that "Young Germany": "Scholars are now unanimous in applying the proud name 'young Germany' to all those who were dauntless and foolish enough to reveal their deepest subjectivity, their most audacious emotions before an audience whose critical standards put even the most righteous soul in danger of being misjudged, and no one can be sure"— note the jump into the present tense—"that today or tomorrow he will not be stamped a traitor. The absurdity of utilitarian criticism that says 'roses are pretty, but I shall praise the chamomile that renders such valuable services when we have a cold' is too great for me to go into it at any length here; I am thinking chiefly of the approach that seeks to congeal the author's every fleeting feeling into a rigid dogma...."

When the conflict arose, one could almost call it a collision between a strong emotion and a dogmatic ideology. It came unexpectedly. Both Gutzkow and Laube were associated with Cotta's journal; Gutzkow, in particular, had quite a close relationship with Menzel. This is echoed in a polemical settling of scores that followed their falling out, when Gutzkow wrote: "For years I have attempted to acquaint Menzel with the younger literary generation. I never would have believed that so vigorous a man could lapse into stagnation, concerned with nothing but extracting pecuniary advantages from the excitable Stuttgart book industry." As recently as 1834, Menzel had sung the praises of Gutzkow's novel *Maha Guru, Geschichte eines Gottes* (Maha Guru, Tale of a God—a bizarre piece of exoticism). What triggered the aggressive volte-face was two works by Gutzkow which

appeared in 1835—his novel *Wally die Zweiflerin* (Wally the
Doubter) and his preface to a new edition of Friedrich
Schleiermacher's *Vertraute Briefe über Schlegel's Lucinde*
(Confidential Letters on Schlegel's Lucinde). They must
have come as a genuine shock to Menzel; the demand for
liberality in matters of love, a plea whose then-radical nature
we can barely conceive of today, was for him a threatening
subversion of society as a whole, and he raged against that
"licentious poetry that seeks only to tempt toward evil sin,
or to excuse it, that seeks to make of a base vice a noble
virtue, that babbles about a 'religion of lust,' as does Friedrich
Schlegel, or that regards it as the culmination of female edi-
fication when young girls are ashamed of shame, as Herr
Gutzkow would have it. . . . Do not befoul places of purity,
do not desecrate with your revolting vices the altar and the
salon"—a staggering juxtaposition—"in which hospitality
receives you!"

Today, the accusations of blasphemy and moral corruption merely seem bizarre; even at the time they must have
sounded foolish to an unbiased observer. In actual fact,
Gutzkow's failed novel displays an emphatic if clumsily conceived sense of ethics, and one is forced to agree with Friedrich Hebbel, surely an unimpeachable witness, when he
notes in his diary: "I have now read Guzkow's *Wally*, which
I only skimmed when it first appeared. How was it possible

for this book to be so perfidiously maligned and its author pilloried? It most certainly is not—as claimed by vile Menzel, whom I have only now come to despise—the product of vanity and strutting sensuality; it is suffused by the spirit of truth, and every page contains an experience for the mind. I do not seek to defend it from a poetic perspective, but even here it is not the intention that deserves criticism, but the unsatisfactory execution." The vanished debate, with its pros and contras, cannot be reconstructed here. But to give a sense of the tone of Menzel's screed, it begins: "I regret that I was incapable of holding Herr Gutzkow to the path of virtue and honor that he once followed." Now, he writes, the author has sinned, now Menzel must intervene, for "Herr Gutzkow is threatening us with a new literary review on a grand scale, a powerful organ of the so-called Young Germany that aims to work great wonders and reshape everything in old Germany.—But I will set my foot in your muck, well knowing that I sully myself. With my foot I will crush the head of the snake that warms itself in the manure of lust." In the quarrel over this novel by Gutzkow, who challenged Menzel in vain to a duel, Menzel presented himself as the champion of a certain view of "morality." His review of *Wally* is entitled "Immoral Literature." As is so often the case, his intellectual stance is limned much more vividly by what he hates than by his descriptions of what is "positive." The contours of Menzel's hatred are revealed with particular clarity in his condemnation of Gutzkow's "immorality." Here emerges a panic-stricken loathing of all that is erotic; above all, Menzel sees eroticism as something that undermines the foundations of the state. The other, the greatest, earliest, most enduring object of Menzel's hatred is Goethe.

... old man, let me tell you openly,
From your past doings you seem
Neither a demigod nor an enthusiast, but a swine.

—EDUARD MÖRIKE, "The Tale of the Confident Man"

With the publication of the two-volume *Die deutsche Literatur* in 1828, Menzel became widely known as Goethe's detractor; he had begun his attacks in 1824–1825 in *Europäische Blätter*. Here we see some of the same catchwords as in the polemic against "Young Germany": Goethe is *"entartet"* (degenerate—this is where that peculiar, poisoned word truly seems to start its career); Goethe is a hedonistic egotist; Goethe is "demoralized." The target of these attacks learned about them from the composer Carl Friedrich Zelter, the great pen friend of his older years, in June 1828; for the most part he disregarded them, noting in a letter that he was perfectly entitled to "ignore everything aimed against me." There are but faint traces of a satiric rebuttal; Goethe's posthumous papers contain a *xenion* in which Menzel is bracketed together with another of Goethe's critics, the Baltic writer Garlieb Merkel (quite a different type, though, than Menzel): "They are kindred spirits, / The boar and the pig; / In the end Herr Menzel's nothing / but a Merkel drawn big."

In his manifesto from 1829, Menzel listed "Goethomania" among the aberrations to be combated. He was the most influential exponent of his era's Goethophobia (though for a long while this placed him in a paradoxical alliance with the Young Germans whom he later antagonized; they too tended to see Goethe in a peculiar double role—as a flunky of the princes, and as a Francophile and the recipient of a medal from Napoleon—at any rate as a man who refused to recognize the nationalistic imperatives of that historic hour). For us the literary canon, at least up until the late nineteenth century, presents itself as a fixed, well-ordered whole, something we take for granted, almost like a natural phenomenon, and we must exert our imaginations to reconstruct how controversial this canon of our classics actually was, how precarious, how historically contingent.

In the mid-nineteenth-century Goethe's reputation had reached an absolute nadir, while Schiller's star was rising (typically, Menzel was quite active in the friends' association for Stuttgart's Schiller memorial). Not until around 1875—that is, shortly after Menzel's death—was Goethe's renown more securely reestablished, waxing again while Schiller was treated with increasing disdain. Indeed, Schiller's reputation has not yet recovered from the proudly moralistic nineteenth century's insistence on praising him as a highly moral poet, in contrast to the "demoralized" Goethe. For the modern period, this was a death sentence; Nietzsche called him the "moral trumpeter of Säckingen."

Goethe, then, was immoral. It is especially important for us to recall that for a long time, in many circles, there was a deeply felt sense that Goethe was not really a good German (and thus, of course, not a great writer). We can seek to grasp this historical sentiment, for which Menzel was in large part responsible, by way of a small detour—citing an author who had nothing in common with the patriotic or *völkisch* literature that orchestrated the contempt and hatred of Goethe. But he once noted an odd little experience in his travel diary, one so exquisite that it must be cited at length. It was July 14, 1912, the author was in the Harz mountains, at a sanatorium strongly influenced by the life reform movement. He was lying "in the grass when the man from the 'Christian

Community' (tall, handsome body, sunburned, pointed beard, happy appearance) walked from the place where he reads" (several days previously our author had seen him lying on the grass, "three Bibles open before him, and tak[ing] notes") "to the dressing-cabin; I followed him unsuspectingly with my eyes, but instead of returning to his place he came in my direction, I closed my eyes, but he was already introducing himself: Hitzer, land surveyor, and gave me four pamphlets as reading matter for Sunday.... I read a little in them and then went back to him and, hesitant because of the respect in which I held him" (our author is surely one of the most courteous people of his century) "tried to make it clear why there was no prospect of grace for me at present. Exercising a beautiful mastery over every word, something that only sincerity makes possible, he discussed this with me for an hour and a half...." The land surveyor warns against "Unhappy Goethe, who made so many other people unhappy."

It is odd that Franz Kafka should fall into the hands of a land surveyor, of all people, but after all, here at the Jungborn Naturopathic Sanatorium, several weeks after visiting Weimar, he also met a Breslau civil servant by the name of Friedrich Schiller. And in his sanatorium conversations his preoccupation with Goethe, which had lately intensified (as one can read in his diary, it was typically and touchingly mingled with an awkward flirtation with the daughter of the Goethehaus custodian), must have emerged in such a way that Herr Hitzer felt called upon to voice his warning against Goethe. The remarkable thing is not so much that Goethe is regarded as "unhappy," which might make a certain kind of sense from the perspective of this sun-tanned Bible reader; the astonishing notion is that Goethe should have made many people unhappy.

This reflects a conception of the great author and his influence that is now lost to us, a conception owing much to Menzel: that great writers and thinkers are supposed to be role models, champions of morality. Nowadays it would hardly occur to us to attempt to live according to the works of a poet, however revered, much less seek a model for our own life in his biography. But that was all the rage in the late nineteenth century, and for a long time thereafter; the classic articulation of this attitude is the then-legendary work *Rembrandt als Erzieher* (Rembrandt as a Pedagogue) by an author, Julius Langbehn, who must indeed be described as *völkisch*. Once an artist, a writer, a thinker has been pinned down to this noble profession, the almost automatic result is harsh censure of those problematic features of his life whose exemplary quality is painfully lacking. With his moralistic criticism of Goethe's supposedly dissolute lifestyle, his coldness, his ingratitude and emotional reserve, and above all his lack of German feeling, Menzel played a major role in shaping this traditional discourse.

Certainly his antagonism must be seen in the context of the central importance of the term "national literature" for Menzel, a term whose objective and descriptive nature (national literature is the literature of a linguistic community) was displaced by the increasingly shrill pathos of political and pedagogical demands: national literature as the instrument that must edify the nation, confronting it with the great historical destiny that is its due, and obliged to see to its moral stability. Ever since 1827 this ideological notion had been shadowed by another concept, one which Goethe had articulated and emphatically championed: that of world literature. "National literature is now rather an unmeaning term;" we read in Eckermann, "the epoch of world literature is at hand, and everyone must strive to hasten its approach." Goethe does say in a letter to Adolph Friedrich Carl Streckfuss, a Berlin civil servant and an important translator, that "The German can and should be most active in this respect; he has a fine part to play in this great mutual approach." But in his *Maxims and Reflections* we read: "Now that the concept of world literature is on the way in, the German, if you look closely, has most to lose: he will do well to think carefully about this warning."

Goethe's stance regarding the question of post-national

politics and culture is expressed most clearly and startlingly in a passage of Eckermann's *Conversations* for which the nationalists never forgave him. Incidentally, Oskar Loerke courageously cited it in 1940 in his preface for an edition of Goethe's *Campaign in France*: "And some will recall his"— Goethe's—"avowal from the year 1830 that there is a degree 'where one stands to a certain extent above nations, and feels the weal or woe of a neighboring people, as if it had happened to one's own.'" Let us cite the passage, from March 14, 1830, at somewhat greater length: first Goethe expressed measured praise of the patriotic poet Theodor Körner (the one with the famous footnote in his poem "Thou Sword in my Left Hand": *"At 'Hurrah!' there is a rattling of swords"); Goethe says: "His war-songs suit him perfectly. But to me, who am not of a warlike nature, and who have no warlike sense, war-songs would have been a mask which would have fitted my face very badly. I have never affected anything in my poetry." And then: "How could I write songs of hatred without hating! And, between ourselves, I did not hate the French, although I thanked God that we were free from them. How could I, to whom culture and barbarism are alone of importance, hate a nation which is among the most cultivated of the earth, and to which I owe so great a part of my own cultivation? Altogether," continued Goethe, "national hatred is something peculiar. You will always find it strongest and most violent where there is the lowest degree of culture. But there is a degree where it vanishes altogether, and where one stands to a certain extent above nations, and feels the weal or woe of a neighboring people, as if it had happened to one's own. This degree of culture was conformable to my nature, and I had become strengthened in it long before I had reached my sixtieth year." Goethe's serene claim to a position of his own at a time of nationalist uproar was unendurable for Menzel, as was his view that culture and barbarism were alone of importance—and for Menzel's era Goethe's audacious sense of culture included far too much eroticism.

Menzel, by contrast, as a critical reviewer and censor, operated from a national standpoint that presupposed a German *Volksgeist*, a national spirit conceived as an unbroken continuity from the Germanic tribes down to the nineteenth century and defined in opposition to "Roman cunning and lies"—whereby "what is Roman" is likewise seen as a virtually identical thing from the time of Arminius down to the contemporary French. Menzel was so aggressive in his Christianity, and so reactionary a Christian, that the novelist Ida, Countess von Hahn-Hahn, much read at the time, asked him wistfully in a letter from 1856, "Ah, I beg you, why are you not a Catholic?" That was based on a misapprehension; Menzel was and would remain rabidly

Protestant, polemicizing against the Jesuits and in many ways anticipating Bismarck's *Kulturkampf*. In its internationality, the papal church of Catholicism was, for him, a further embodiment of "what is Roman," a calamity for Germany.

These sorts of ambitious historical constructions, unthinkingly relying on categories such as "what is German" to label millennia of complex processes and shifts, were a common feature of the time. Menzel, however, had reached a point at which national character could apparently be evoked only hand in hand with xenophobia and racism. In the third volume of *Deutsche Dichtung*, Menzel attempts a characterization of the recent past: "The Catholic church had not yet recovered from the terrible disruptions of Josephinism and Napoleonism and had come under pressure from the state, which for a long while ensured the suppression of its spirit. The Protestant church had nearly been dissolved by rationalism and open unbelief. Hegel announced to Prussia's youth that man himself was God. Fear of God no longer offered any moral stability. Patriotism, the vessel of moral nobility, was officially forbidden as well. Thus unprecedented moral corruption and perfidy arose in the press.—It was not surprising that amidst this general neglect and contempt of the church Christ's oldest enemies, the Jews, should make use of a moment so favorable for them.

They emerged from every dark corner, monkey-like, baring
their teeth, grinning and sticking out their tongues to mock
all that had been sacred to Christians, infernal Cercopes
that for centuries, half-crushed and hiding in the dark
beneath the heavy roof beams of the Gothic church, had
merely peered out shyly, but now, with an impudent salto
mortale, leaped into the midst of the dissolute congregation
and seduced them to worship the Golden Calf and deify
concupiscence." In ancient mythology, the Cercopes are an
especially guileful tribe transformed into monkeys by Zeus
to punish a brazen deception. One cannot deny that this
passage has a certain stylistic verve, and great vividness. Here
a literary criticism that thinks and argues in nationalistic
terms has found its innermost essence: the mad, racist rejection of all that is "foreign."

It seems obvious that Menzel's anti-Semitism, so vividly
revealed here, corresponds to his "scourging of the French"
or, as Börne put it in an article written in French, the "gal-
lophobie de M. Menzel." This attack on all that is French is
not merely patriotic; it also reflects the self-positioning of
an anti-Enlightenment intellectual who views the world
with the eyes of a *Kulturkampf* Protestant and a Teutono-
phile. In this way, as a "case study" in literary history, Menzel
brings together certain typical features of his time in
especially striking form; he presents, as it were, a phenotype

of his era's intellectual psychopathology. The problematic aspect of Menzel's work does not lie in the sweeping aspirations that he holds, in this sense a true heir to both Classicism and Romanticism, for literary criticism: the aspirations of using it as a forum for a comprehensive criticism of German life as a whole. It lies in his attempt, increasingly dogmatic and ultimately descending into blind rage, to use the cudgels of chauvinism and fundamentalist religion to force through the totality of a perspective which he cannot achieve intellectually. The longer he fails to provide a positive definition of what is "German," the more aggressively he defines it in negative terms, by way of rejection—through Francophobia, anti-Semitism.

Arno Schmidt, whose references to Menzel have been compiled by Thomas Lautwein in an instructive essay in the *Bargfelder Bote*, made intensive use of the great works of literary history written by this rabid ideologue. He called him a man "of demonic erudition, which ensures the importance of his 3-volume *German Poetry*; for one thing because he provides a brief summary of each book, with the names of the main characters—a forerunner of the *Oxford Companion*—and then because his verdicts are so reliably wrong that each and every book he branded as heretical can be read with pleasure to this day." That is a melancholy epitaph for a once-powerful, indeed over-powerful critic. But it is true:

there is almost no way Menzel can instruct us now except *ex negativo*. That goes for his specific judgments on contemporary literature, and it goes for his overall conception of literary criticism. It is a warning sign. Those facing the minefield of literature and its criticism may, under certain circumstances, value such a sign more highly than a monument to one more dignified or congenial.

"I lie in fetters forged by me"
Wagner's Contradiction-Crossed Plan for the *Valkyrie*

Two ravens sit on Odin's shoulders, and bring to his ears all that they hear and see. Their names are Hugin and Munin. At dawn he sends them out to fly over the whole world, and they come back at breakfast time. Thus he gets information about many things, and hence he is called Rafnagud (raven-god).

—Snorri Sturluson, *Gylfaginning* xxxviii

In the *ring*, Wagner created one of the unlikeliest of deities. Wotan knows many things, almost everything, but what good does it do him? He works magic; according to tradition, he invented the runes. When he walks the world incognito, what does he see, what does he hear, what does he ponder on his lonely wanderings? He is entangled in plans that contradict one another. At an unforeseen moment in *Faust* we're reminded of him: the mistress of the witch's kitchen, astonished and delighted, recognizes the devil, whom at first she had failed to identify in his harmless incarnation. And then she asks: "Where are your two ravens?" There is a line leading from Wotan to Mephisto. From the outset Wotan, the highest god, is a similarly shifty strategist, an intriguer. While the crafty Mephisto does not stumble until the very end of the play—even here, some interpreters feel, he is only tripped up by an unfair gimmick of grace, having actually won his bet—Wotan, ensnared from the very start of the *Ring* in a contract he cannot fulfill, is the victim of his own improvisations, all of which have more ramifications than he can foresee.

In the virtually inextricable difficulties of the beginning of the story in *Rheingold*, Loge comes to his rescue. But *The Valkyrie* finds Wotan—having abandoned "in deep dejection" the plan to base his world's salvation on the Wälsungs' incest—confronted with utterly unexpected insubordination: the revolt of the Valkyrie. The creator no longer recognizes his creature. In such situations our sympathies are with the creature; we celebrate the rebellion of Prometheus. ("The most eminent saint and martyr in the philosophical calendar," according to Marx. Prometheus too was held prisoner on a rock.) This distant comparison points out something else as well: the qualities which Greek myth ascribes to the rebellious creature—inventiveness, guile, the devising of ever-new ideas—are largely the privilege of the god Wotan himself. The fact that one character in the *Ring of the*

Nibelung, namely Loge, represents guile par excellence all too easily obscures the extent of Wotan's own wiles, preoccupied as he is with secret plans. The Valkyries are part of another grand plan: to gather the host of the dead for the battle at the end of time. Their siring was strategic. Wotan doesn't tinker with bits of corpses like a certain other dubious nineteenth-century creator, Dr. Frankenstein, but a carrion stench pervades his plans. He sires the Valkyries as gatherers of corpses. One of the most remarkable phenomena of Wilhelminism, until World War I rendered this particular delusion impossible, was the extent to which the era sought to view the battlefield purely as the scene of decorative heroism. Wilhelm Trübner's lost painting *Kaiser Wilhelm I. und der Kronprinz auf dem Schlachtfeld von Walküren begrüßt* (Kaiser Wilhelm I and the Crown Prince Greeted on the Battlefield by Valkyries, 1897, a belated patriotic response to the events of 1870–71) completely misconstrues the nature of the Valkyries. The old saga, with all its partiality for heroism, recognized the horror of battle. The Valkyries are terrible, menacing apparitions; in his *Deutsche Mythologie* (German Mythology, chapter 16) Jacob Grimm speculates, on the basis of Anglo-Saxon sources, that they were regarded as figures that resembled the Greek Gorgons. Then Brünnhilde would have the head of Medusa.

I gave simple fucking instructions!

—STEVE BUSCEMI in *Fargo* (1996), by Joel and Ethan Coen

Brünnhilde is disobedient. The creature rebels against the creator; this is one of the oldest stories in existence. And as always the god is uncomprehending: can it be "that e'en thou, my creature, dost meet me with scorn?"

We value myths of insubordination. All the same, Brünnhilde's disobedience is a very peculiar thing. The Valkyries are utterly instrumental creatures, servants of the battleruler; they belong to Wotan just as the Wild Host (which old legends refer to as the *"wütende"* [furious], Wotan's Host) belongs to the Wild Hunter. They must follow him as the Erlkönig's daughters follow their father. They have a single purpose before which all else pales to insignificance: the Valkyries belong to death. They determine victory and defeat, but they celebrate battle only because it yields the corpses to populate Valhalla. What interests them is not the victor, it is the brave man killed in action; he provides suitable "human material." They are monofunctional figures of glory or horror to whom only Wagner gives names (all too artful ones, in their historicizing Germanicism). They were never permitted to be individuals.

The Brothers Grimm, in the second volume of their

dictionary under *brünne* (coat of mail), offer one of their frequent commentaries that go beyond the purely objective: "a beautiful word, stemming from *brinnen*, to gleam, thus also related to *braun* [brown], gleaming, shining, which ought to have been kept in living use instead of *panzer* [armor]." It was not kept in use, so when we think of "Brünn-hilde," we should remind ourselves of this "armor." Like her sisters Gerhilde, Schwertleite, Helmwige—whose names refer to spears, swords, helmets respectively—she is named after weaponry, indeed, she is nothing but a weapon.

The singular "Valkyrie" as an opera title is strange in itself. This strangeness reflects the violence with which Wagner inserted, indeed forced the tale of an Icelandic queen desired by the Burgundian ruler into the apocalyptic mythos of Wotan's corpse-hoarding battle-maidens. The Valkyries are really conceivable only in the plural. James Ensor—in one of many late-nineteenth-century manifestations of Wag-nermania, from Fantin-Latour to Beardsley—painted them as a flying host of spear-carrying stick figures, swirling over the city like witches riding to the Sabbath (*The Ride of the Valkyries*, ca. 1888). Even the more pathos-laden depictions of Valkyries, produced in numerous variants by the painters of the era, have in common the eschewal of individuation, depicting either a collective or a type. Now Brünnhilde sud-denly emerges as a personality with a resolute will of her own.

She claims through her very disobedience to do her father's will, his true will; she reminds him of what he intended before Fricka's intervention forced him to change his plans. But that is not what Wotan raised her for. His entire plan for siring and training the Valkyries was based on the assumption that the whole troop would function unthinkingly. Now his orders have been refused.

Antigone knew nothing of politics;—she loved.

—RICHARD WAGNER, *Opera and Drama* (Part II)

Where does a daughter figure, sworn to obedience, find this boundless source of resistance? (A power of denial which the Valkyrie will display once again in the last part of the *Ring*—with her passionate refusal when a sister shows her the way to save the world from destruction: she need only return Siegfried's love token, the Ring, to the Rhine maidens.... She declines, "though into ruins / Walhall's splendor should fall!") The opera offers the rather sentimental explanation that she is "hastily" overwhelmed by pity for Sieglinde. In fact her rebellion seems to have a completely different origin. Its power emerges from the crevices and interstices of the complicated mythology Wagner created, more of a surrealistic bricolage than one would at first imagine. Above all it seems to stem from a Bluebeard's chamber, anxiously barred and bolted by Wagner, holding certain passages from the tenth chapter of the *Song of the Nibelungs*. For in its dreamlike power Wagner's convoluted mythos also lives from the tales he *doesn't* tell, the ones he discarded. He completely rearranged, transposed, custom-tailored the *Song of the Nibelungs*, crossing it with ancient Nordic sagas of gods and heroes to produce something utterly new. And the epic contains passages which, though he does not use them, constantly resonate in the consciousness of the *Ring*'s listeners as peculiar interferences. One of these suppressed figurations is that of Brünnhilde as a ruler, as a woman of demonic autonomy, as an unmastered erotic challenge. In the *Song of the Nibelungs*, we first hear of her as a distant queen, desirable and lethal: confrontation means death for all suitors who lose the contest. This is an ancient feature of fairytales and myths, but Brünnhilde vanquishes her suitors not by posing riddles (like Turandot), nor by her swiftness (like Atalanta), nor by assigning tests which she observes from afar—she prevails through her own boundless and ready powers. The extent of these powers is revealed by one of the key episodes (X, 637 ff., 648–650) in the *Song of the Nibelungs*. On the wooing journey to Iceland Siegfried, under his cloak of invisibility, helped Gunther vanquish Brünnhilde; the king can now marry the woman of his desire. But the wedding night in Worms turns into a nightmarish catastrophe. The bride resists Gunther's advances, demanding that he first explain a mystery to her. At the wedding, Gunther's sister Kriemhild was married to Siegfried (in reward for his secret assistance), and this unprecedented, indeed mortifying alliance between the king's sister and a vassal makes Brünnhilde suspicious and vaguely jealous. Gunther refuses to answer, and tries to force her, but— the next day, upon Siegfried's inquiries, he relates the incident, which is not without a certain cruel humor—his wife ties him up with her belt (*"do ich si wânde minnen / vil sêre si mich bant"*) and hangs him from a nail high up on the wall, where he dangles anxiously until morning. *"Dâ hieng ich angestlîchen / di naht unz an den tag."*

The Romantic painter Johann Heinrich Füssli immersed himself in the *Song of the Nibelungs* and left a vast cycle of drawings and paintings based upon it; if he had pursued the endeavor as systematically as he compiled entire galleries of illustrations for Milton and Shakespeare, no doubt it would have stood as his magnum opus. Of his many remarkable compositions ("Siegfried Bathing in the Blood of the Dragon"), one is especially astonishing. With particular intensity, the great fetishist and great artist, guided by the sadomasochistic fantasies apparent in many of his works, depicted a motif which no other visual artist appears to have rendered: Gunther hanging from the wall (1817). In the foreground, on the upper right, the king—muscular, but no match for this woman—hangs naked from a fetter that clasps both hands and both feet. Brünnhilde, in an attitude that could almost be a direct allusion to David's *Madame Récamier*, reclines on a daybed in the back, on the left, in translucent robes and with one of those fantastically piled-up hairdos that fascinated the keenly fetishistic Füssli. With a smile she regards the helpless man whose genitals, invisible to the viewer, are exposed to her gaze. The image has the effect of an intense meditation on the intimacy that bonds those who participate in this sort of humiliating staged violence. Gunther will not manage to escape the spell of the bridal chamber until the invisible Siegfried takes his place once again.

In Wagner's telling of the myth, only fragments of this situation remain, but the missing things stir in the background. Siegfried's rape of Brünnhilde, wearing Gunther's cloak of invisibility, is presented in *The Twilight of the Gods*—with the threatening euphemism "Now art thou mine... show me the way to thy chamber!"—but Gunther's prior humiliation is expunged. In both narratives, only a single, select man can subjugate this women (nothing defines

Siegfried so sharply as his ability, shared by no other man, to bed Brünnhilde), but her mockery of men is eliminated. Under the cloak of Wagner's textual revisions, this could provide the driving power behind Brünnhilde's "impudence" in confronting Wotan.

Why does what goes untold continue as part of the story? When Ibsen, in an anecdote recorded by Arnold Hauser, "was once asked why his Nora from *A Doll's House* had such a foreign-sounding name, he answered that she was named after her grandmother who was Italian. Her real name was Eleonora, but she had been pampered as a child and called Nora. To the objection that all this played no part in the play itself, he replied in amazement: 'But facts are still facts.'" Exquisite evidence for the profound reveries of a writer, and, what is more, for the truth about all complex narratives: they rest upon an invisible foundation of the untold. This is especially true of the *Ring*; the rubble of the forerunner narratives which Wagner used as a quarry protrudes into it deeply and in unexpected places. This adds to its sublime, bewildering complexity. The music so magnificently—and, if one follows the densely woven web of leitmotifs, so obsessively—unifies the whole complicated narrative of the *Ring of the Nibelung* that only closer examination of the plot logic reveals how confused and contradictory it is. Wagner mulled over the *Ring* for a quarter of a century, but the result was not a seamless work—fortunately, for this adds to the brilliantly compelling, dreamlike power of the text and the action.

G. K. Chesterton astutely observed with regard to Charles Dickens's grotesquely vital and sinister characters that there is a certain mystery about these novels, one not adequately clarified by the final resolution of the intrigues that make up the plot—it is as though the characters know something that remains unknown not only to the reader, but to the author himself. In the *Ring*, darkly alluding to past events and fears of the future, the characters seem to tell of something that the audience does not know, something that confuses even the author. It is the productive confusion of the great imagination.

Then make yourself a second plan,
then let the whole thing drop.
—BERTOLT BRECHT, *The Threepenny Opera*

Wotan's plans come to naught; that is what sets in motion the plot of the *Ring*. It is odd that Wagner dresses the actual reason for the stymieing of Wotan's Wälsung project—Fricka's jealous indignation—in the trivial garb of a marital row

("The wonted storm, the wonted strife!"). And yet this has its own logic: in certain circumstances, great plans can be thwarted by trifles.

But the changed plan—that Siegmund and Sieglinde must die—comes up against a great force: Brünnhilde's revolt. The energy that drives her seems to burst forth because it is dammed up elsewhere. In Wagner's work, the Valkyrie Brünnhilde is not released from the game of intrigue, of invisibility and rape, but she has been deprived of the irrepressible, mocking power which let her hang Gunther from the nail. (Meanwhile, the Kriemhild of the *Song of the Nibelungs* whom Siegfried's death leaves inconsolable, whose thirst for blood sets in motion "Der Nibelunge Nôt," the fall of the Nibelungs, appears only as the tender, demure, sketchy figure of Gutrune, "Gunther's gentle sister.") Does this power reemerge as the "impudent" obstinacy of the Valkyrie who flouts her regimented battle orders and confronts her father? Wotan's plans are thwarted by the force of this obstinacy that so unexpectedly reveals itself in Brünnhilde, his creature—they are thwarted, one might say, by the residuum of the stifled narrative context, by all that Wagner's eclectic approach to the *Song of the Nibelungs* sought to ignore and that now, in a sort of resurgence of the suppressed, suddenly erupts: a woman's indomitable self-will. What in the *Song of the Nibelungs* is embedded in a manifestly sexual context is de-eroticized in the *Ring* and immersed in a pathos of pity that has echoes of Schopenhauer. But her unyieldingness remains as an identifying feature.

Is Wagner Wotan, is Wotan Wagner? Of course the question is nonsensical one way or the other. We could say that in one respect Wagner fares as Wotan does. In planning this gigantic work, he makes one false start after another, becoming as ensnared in his plans as the god does. But in the process he creates a world. "I lie in fetters forged by me"—the wording and the situation have the aesthetically pleasing coherence of a rounded, self-contained context. The failure of great plans compellingly shapes the course of events.

Max Eyth and the Specter of Technology

"Dear me," said Mr. Grewgious, peeping in, "it's like looking down the throat of old time."

—CHARLES DICKENS, *The Mystery of Edwin Drood*

THE NINETEENTH century is far removed from us. The twentieth century lies in between, regarding us with quite a remote gaze itself. And yet we must go back to the nineteenth century to grasp some little part of the chain of unsolved—unsolvable?—problems we drag along behind us, for it is there that everything begins. It is the beginning of that rapid technological progress we so readily describe as breathtaking, forgetting what language seeks to express with this image—that above a certain speed, one is literally unable to breathe. But it is also the beginning of the dilemma which, more than any other, has shaped all the times to come, including our insouciant era: the discrepancy between our technological capabilities and what our mind is truly able to penetrate, between our inventiveness and our moral imagination, between what we are able to picture *somehow*, that is, everything, and what we are *truly* able to picture, to face in our mind's eye with all its consequences—that is, hardly anything anymore. To gaze back at the nineteenth century is to confront an era which—as we eye the quaint illustrations in its family journals, as we read its poems— easily inspires a kind of sentimental scorn. And yet in this era's depths lie all the things that grin at us today with the Medusa's gaze of the unsolvable problem.

It often makes sense to approach an era by focusing on a characteristic figure from the margins rather than an outstanding major personality. Max Eyth was a man of some importance, but he was neither a truly brilliant innovator nor a great writer. He is noteworthy for his fusion of clear-sightedness with naivety, and especially of bourgeois sobriety with an almost ecstatic, sensual passion for technology. What was he? An engineer who wrote a once widely read autobiography, *Hinter Pflug und Schraubstock* (At the Plow and the Vise), as well as novels: *Der Kampf um die Cheopspyramide* (The Battle for the Great Pyramid), *Der Schneider von Ulm* (The Tailor of Ulm). "Max Eyth, like many a son from a Swabian family, was supposed to become a pastor," begins the brief sketch of the author in the Marbach catalogue *Literatur im Industriezeitalter* (Literature in the Industrial Age, 1987), only to continue, like an edifying story from a late-Enlightenment-era primer: "The noise of a hammer mill was what strengthened in him the resolution, even as a child, to become an engineer." He was born in 1836 in Kirchheim unter Teck; when he was five, the family moved to Schöntal an der Jagst, where his father had become a professor at the theological seminary. Max was privately educated by his father before attending the seminary himself and spending half a year at the middle school in Heilbronn in preparation for his engineering studies, which he began in 1852 at the polytechnic university in Stuttgart. At the age of twenty-one he went to work for several years at a steam engine factory in Berg near Stuttgart, then traveled to England, where he met John Fowler, the pioneer of the steam plow, who had single-handedly run the company John Fowler & Co. in Leeds since 1863. After spending 1863–1866 in Egypt, working as chief engineer in the service of an uncle of the viceroy, from 1866–1882 Eyth, "steam plow missionary" (as the literature about him inevitably puts it) for the Fowler company, for which he also made various important inventions, travelled through nearly all of Europe and half the world—to the United States and Russia, back to Egypt, and to Turkey, Trinidad, Panama, and Peru. After 1882, Eyth founded and organized the German Agricultural Society, acting as its president until 1896. Numerous honors and titles round out the picture of a successful and affluent life, which ended in Ulm in 1906.

Eyth was an inventor and entrepreneur and, to the extent of his abilities, a writer and poet.

Revolutionary inventions were made early on in human history, and everyone can name a few upon brief reflection— the wheel, the taming of fire, the breeding of high-yield grains. Over the following centuries and millennia, radically revolutionary inventions—gunpowder, printing—gradually increased. Incidentally, historians inform us that even certain seemingly obscure inventions have radically altered human history, for instance the development of the stirrup, which according to one school of historians shaped the course of the entire Middle Ages. But in the nineteenth century a different tempo of change set in—while at the same time the inertia of the old remained considerable. Focusing on Max Eyth means attempting, through the prism of biography, to gaze back at an era that was already jolted by the radical upheavals of technology, but still had some sense of a *longue durée*, especially in the vast rural provinces where little had changed for half a millennium or even more. The pathos of early Soviet novels with titles such as *Virgin Soil Upturned* reflects the degree to which the modern era, not only under socialism, heroicized the technological changes that agriculture underwent. Max Eyth's steam plows are the forerunners of the tractors that dug the furrows from which a new society was supposed to grow. At one time the word "steam plow"

must have seemed very odd, fusing as it did the latest technology with something extremely archaic, the steam engine
and the plow. The plow is an ancient object. For a long time
it was one of those things that still connect us directly to
antiquity, like a coin, a sandal, a sundial, a dog, a bunch of
grapes. Steam power was the signature of innovative technological modernity. As a heterogeneous compound word, the
steam plow is something like an electric toothbrush, whose
radical drollness we have already ceased to perceive, or (taking
a random invention to make my point), an atomic frying pan.

*. . . the silent, majestic river, upon whose bank, in the evening, Death
speeds along on a bicycle.*
—GIOVANNINO GUARESCHI, *Mondo piccolo: Don Camillo*
(1948)

In fact, the stuffily bourgeois figure of Max Eyth, who evokes
all the cozy security of his age with the magisterial, bewhis-
kered face of his late photographs, stands for one of the most
powerful archetypes of modernity, the inventor. This figure
always seems compromised in some way. When we say
"inventor," popular mythology suggests an embellishing

adjective: the "crazy" inventor, as Gyro Gearloose of Duck-
burg is called by his neighbors. In France he has a superficially harmless, yet vaguely disturbing name: there he is
known as Géo Trouvetout. An inventor is someone who
discovers everything. What is disturbing, of course, is that
"everything." If there is nothing the inventor is not prepared
to invent, then (in current parlance) we have a problem.
The willingness to produce everything that could possibly
be conceived of—as articulated in Leonardo da Vinci's
famous letter to the Duke of Milan—is the pride and shame
of the inventor. Does this contradiction hold even for an
invention like the steam plow, so manifestly beneficial, the
vanquisher of hunger? The line begun by Eyth's steam plows
leads directly to the vast wheat fields that stretched to the
horizon; in the capitalist American Midwest and the communist Soviet Union's kolkhozes it subverts nature, causing
the dust storms that the impoverished farmers flee in *Grapes
of Wrath*, and creating the steppes and deserts that have con-
quered broad swathes of what was once Soviet farmland.

Though some signs of the gathering storm were apparent,
Max Eyth did not live to see the unclouded fantasies of
progress come to an end. He is fascinating precisely as the
representative of an age that still celebrated technology in
strangely bucolic fashion, extolling and taming it at the great
World Expositions. Eyth often expressed skepticism about

these expositions, but that concerned their utility for him as an exhibitor. In their content, these palaces of commodities precisely reflected his vision of the onward march of technology. For Walter Benjamin, the world exhibitions take a central place in his unfinished magnum opus, the so-called Arcades Project, one early incarnation of which was the essay "Paris, Capital of the Nineteenth Century." These dazzlingly illuminated palaces with their phantasmagorias of commodification seemed to embody the century. Does it make sense to cite so ambitious a theory as Benjamin's in connection with Eyth's work? Oddly, there is something slightly uncanny about Eyth's trusting love of technology that points precisely toward Benjamin's context. With his penchant for describing a factory hall as a "magical cavern," for seeing giants and dwarves everywhere, for gracing workers with descriptions such as "they file in and out, like industrious gnomes at work," and generally using the imagery of a fairy-tale forest to describe the most advanced industrial activity, Eyth establishes a peculiar contradiction. Later, with unerring judgment, he lauded Whitman and Kipling as great poets of technology and praised Adolph Menzel's painting *The Iron-Rolling Mill*; alongside such insights, his own poetry seems especially odd. The poems are touching in their artlessness; of course, they come from an era in which even poetry with much higher aspirations strikes us as unbearably conventional in both form and thinking. There is one noteworthy thing, however: Eyth is fascinated by great size, by records, by the unusual, but behind this lies a passionate attachment to what might be called the simplicity of work. Later the literature of technology would be completely dominated by the penchant for the extraordinary, the intoxication of size, height, speed; the Italian Futurists would fall in love with airplanes and aerial war. There is something mysteriously disarming about Eyth's love for a piece of metal in the vise, caressed with outright sensuality.

Nowadays the steam engine has long since been consigned to the prop room of history; those who can recall seeing steam locomotives in operation, not at nostalgic weekend events but as a regular mode of transport, are forced to realize how old they are. What has vanished with the steam locomotive is a vestige of the visual quality of technological energy. The technical process that sets the steam engine in motion is accessible to the viewer; its nature is evident. Ernst Bloch once noted that steam power marks the last stage of technology that children are still able to mimic in their games—their arm movements imitate the rhythm and accelerating speed of the coupling rods. Buster Keaton transformed this rhythmic motion into one of the most elegant images in film history. The melancholy engineer, sitting lost in thought on his locomotive's coupling

MAX EYTH AND THE SPECTER OF TECHNOLOGY

rod, unexpectedly trundles away with it when someone starts up the engine—rising and falling, he passes out of the picture, and the brilliant actor's famously motionless face seems to say that however surprising this may appear, it is exactly as it must be: this is how the machine moves.

The cover of Eyth's *Hinter Pflug und Schraubstock. Skizzen aus dem Taschenbuch eines Ingenieurs* (At the Plow and the Vise: Sketches from an Engineer's Notebook, 1899), which he designed himself, shows a huge steam plow at work, steered by a figure bearing a remote resemblance to the author. In the upper part of the picture, above the title, a decorative panorama of mountains, pyramids, and industrial chimneys spouting fire and smoke rises from the majestic cloud of steam that billows up from the lower part of the image beneath the title cartouche; in front of this panorama, a train shoots out of a tunnel onto a high bridge—and for no apparent reason the bridge collapses. We behold one of the great motifs of the nineteenth-century imagination—"A bauble, a naught, / What the hand of man hath wrought!" Theodor Fontane wrote in "The Bridge by the Tay," a ballad based on the actual collapse of the Tay Bridge near Dundee in Scotland, the world's longest railway bridge, on December 29, 1879, which caused a train with seventy-five passengers to plunge into the depths. The fascination and the celebration of technology go hand in hand with evocations of catastrophe. Superficially this may seem an irksome matter of duty. Eyth writes: "I do not wish to speak of the catastrophes that are part of our profession, of the firedamp in the coal mines that catapult hundreds of honest, hardworking people into eternity, the collapse of a bridge, a stupendous railway accident, a breach in a dam, the hazards and dangers that surround every step our pioneers take on the path of progress.... It is more gratifying to point out what our activities have bestowed upon the world...." There may be more behind it, though, something resembling a secret sympathy with the catastrophe whose radical upheaval, whose power to reshape might well impress technicians. For if literature is any guide, brilliant engineers are far more often dedicated to the craft of destruction than that of construction.

The twisted ways of Daedalus the old...
—WILLIAM MORRIS, *The Life and Death of Jason*

The crazy inventor mentioned above is a lovably eccentric figure, native to the world of cranks and oddballs of whom German literature, with its tradition of romanticizing parochialism as charming whimsicality, was especially fond. But inventors are not merely crazy, they're often utterly mad. Though Jules Verne and H. G. Wells developed two completely contradictory possibilities for what was later called science fiction, they were unanimous in their fascination with the power generated by technology and science, a power that tends to shade into madness. A *Herrenmensch* gone berserk, the brilliant inventor schemes to conquer the world. In Verne's work, lonely, Byronic figures such as "Robur le Conquérant" and the vengeful Captain Nemo travel high up in the air or far under the sea, and their technological capabilities serve to spread terror. In H. G. Wells's novel *The Invisible Man*, the eponymous protagonist, a doctor who achieved this monstrous breakthrough by experimenting on himself, declares that in his uniqueness he has no choice but to rule the world. "And that Invisible Man . . . must now establish a Reign of Terror. Yes—no doubt it's startling. But I mean it. A Reign of Terror." In the film (Universal, 1933, starring Claude Rains), the Invisible Man pointedly adds: "We'll begin with a reign of terror. A few murders here and there. Murders of great men, murders of little men. Just to show we make no distinction." Over the past few years, it has become more difficult to enjoy this sort of pointed dialogue.

In the Belle Époque, as the mad scientist explores and extends the range of his classic role, he still remains something of a Nietzschean borderline case. The radical skepticism as to whether *any* of us, individuals or humanity as a whole, possess anything resembling the ability to keep pace mentally (rationally and emotionally) with the technological capabilities we ourselves have created was not articulated until the nineteenth century finally ended: during World War I. The writer who most trenchantly expressed the mistrust of the "techno-romantic adventure" was Karl Kraus. Above all, he persistently pointed to one aspect that could be crucial when contemplating our situation: while technology already dwells in the future, our metaphors still use old formulas of kitsch. Language reveals its impotence. Poison gas and flamethrowers are deployed, but Wilhelm II speaks of his sharp-honed sword. There are such things as productive anachronisms, but this one is delusional.

With the end of World War I, which Eyth did not live to see—1906 and 1918 are divided by an epochal caesura, mentally measuring far more than twelve years—we arrive at the period when the world of machines becomes a major theme for novels and plays (in Expressionism) as well as films. In part this is a fashionable phenomenon, but it goes much deeper than that. Seeking the traces of machines in literature, one might not immediately think of Rilke. And yet in the *Sonnets to Orpheus* he writes of the machine:

Nowhere does it stay behind; we cannot escape it at last
as it rules, self-guided, self-oiled, from its silent factory.
It thinks it is life: thinks it does everything best,
though with equal determination it can create or destroy.

We can hardly tell whether the line "self-guided, self-
oiled, from its silent factory" is dominated by unintentional
humor, a brilliant vision of future absurdity or poetic quirks
of assonance. But in German literature it launches an *agon*
waged between inwardness and a hyperbolic modernity
fascinated by the mechanical *à tout prix*—between Rilke
and Brecht.

Doubt had set in long before: when the first mechanical
looms appeared on the scene, Goethe, in *Wilhelm Meister*,
articulated a universal skepticism about the machine age. It
is partly explained in a remark he made to Eckermann (on
October 1, 1828) that shows the full extent of his critical
stance toward the scientific and technological awakening of
the epoch at hand: "We must go slowly and gently [*läßlich*]
to work with nature, if we would get anything out of her."
Läßlich—it is worth reflecting for a moment on this unusual
word—denotes a gesture of care, delicacy, almost of humil-
ity—the willingness to get something, to "get something
out of her," not at all costs, but only if it offers itself. How

innocent and unworldly that seems to us—we live in a completely different world. It is remarkable what clear-sighted
words one finds in nineteenth-century Germany's great
conservative critiques of technology. Karl Leberecht Immer-
mann's novel *Die Epigonen* (The Epigones, 1836), already
reverberating from the noise of the "steam engine furiously
at work" arrives at astonishing locutions, as when factories
are described as "establishments for the artificial satisfaction
of artificial needs." Certainly distinguishing a natural need
from an artificial one is not as simple as this description
suggests; on the other hand, we are now losing hold of the
notion that there could be any distinction at all. The machines
whose mass deployment Eyth so tirelessly promoted produce
bread—and money. And the way in which they produce
bread causes the flow of capital to take very specific routes.
America's naturalistic literature described the stock market
as a jungle, especially in Frank Norris's novel about the wheat
market, *The Pit*. Eyth's propagandistic interventions were
clearly intimately bound up with the global market: after
American cotton production collapsed during the Civil War,
plans were made to establish a competing cotton industry
in Egypt. And Eyth's presentations in the United States were
aimed at an industry that had lost its old stability and the
majority of its workers due to the war and the emancipation
of the slaves. These are just a few small facets, illustrating

selective parts of the complexities in which Eyth's life and work was embedded. But in a strange way, this life from the depths of the nineteenth century tells of our ongoing central dilemma: our infatuated faith in technology.

We are unable to turn around and start our experience of technology afresh. Walter Benjamin's image of the angel of history has never been more apt: the angel would like to pause "to piece together what has been broken." But the storm of so-called progress is caught in his wings, driving him inexorably onwards. When we can no longer simply turn around, what do we do? We can reflect. Certainly we can begin by reminding ourselves that technology continually provides us with things that make daily life easier. In one of his works Arno Schmidt made a short list of the key inventions of what was then the past hundred years: the bicycle, the typewriter, the condom, the telephone, and aspirin. But let us consider that this list, in its meticulous autobiographical calibration, not only expresses gratitude, it is also rooted in a pathos of all that is small and incidental, the fundamentality of daily life, and implicitly in renunciation. No grand gestures, no pathos about changing the world. This is not to state the case for an ethos of utility— nothing can be more necessary than the superfluous. But our postulates for what we wish technology to perform can no longer be articulated with Max Eyth's fundamental faith in progress. He provides us with a fascinating object of study. In this author we discern, as it were, one of the last moments in which an enthusiast was still capable of loving technology without inhibitions, investing this liaison with the noblest hopes for all humanity. Even at the time this was a bit excessive. As though secretly perturbed, the sober Swabian entrepreneur seems to attempt to repair with lyricism what in reality was already cracking up. Here, for one last time, technology, youthfully steaming, progressing in triumph, confronts us as something that is *felt*. In his awkward poems, Max Eyth caresses the machines tenderly. We are already beginning to gaze back yearningly at the industrial labor that was seen for so long as the epitome of alienation, the destruction of human life potential—yearningly, for our society is unable to provide a large segment of its population with work of any kind, and in hindsight the secure assembly-line job appears not as dehumanization but as a guarantee of existential meaning and pride. At a time like this, all early forms of technology and industrial production regain their mystery. In the posthumously published novel *Der Schneider von Ulm* (The tailor of Ulm was a utopian amateur who tried to build a flying apparatus), Eyth explored the failure of the pioneer who, as we like to say, is ahead of his time. Technology as a whole confronts us with a problem: humanity—thinking, feeling humanity—lags behind its (technological) time.

Universal or Particular?
Proust and the Dreyfus Affair

THE DIMENSIONS of this topic, Proust and the Dreyfus affair, make a brief description seem an almost far-fetched undertaking. The greatest cause célèbre of the waning nineteenth century, the event that confronted the Paris correspondent Theodor Herzl with the intransigence of anti-Semitism and turned him into a Zionist, this most convoluted of tales—and one of the longest, most complex novels of the past century.... And, *nota bene*, that tricky little "and," "Proust *and* the Dreyfus affair".... Let us attempt it in the awareness of the endeavor's absurdity.

Ultimately it is impossible to briefly summarize what happened in the Dreyfus affair—not just because of the intrigues, forgeries, and cover-ups that accompanied the investigations and legal proceedings from the start, but also because the tragedy of Captain Dreyfus and his final rehabilitation played out against a background of dizzying political vicissitudes, constant government shake-ups, coalitions, resignations, the toppling of ministers. And all this in the highly charged climate of France's internal conflicts following its defeat by Germany in the war of 1870–71 and the reactionary agitation that threatened the unstable Second Republic on a fundamental level, as a system of government. Very briefly: In 1894 the French army's intelligence section found a memorandum, the notorious *bordereau*, indicating that a high-ranking French officer was supplying the German military attaché with classified information. In December Alfred Dreyfus, an artillery captain from an Alsatian Jewish family who had recently been assigned to the General Staff, was identified as the author and court-martialed as a treasonous spy. On January 5, 1895, he was formally degraded; his epaulettes were torn off, and his sword was broken. This ceremony took place in the courtyard of the École Militaire; no photograph exists, but the scene was imagined countless times in contemporary newspaper illustrations and cartoons. On April 13, 1895, Dreyfus landed on Devil's Island off the coast of French Guiana, where he was imprisoned under conditions verging on torture.

The public discussion soon quieted down, but gradually people convinced of Dreyfus's innocence joined together in a movement to demand a retrial. One key aspect of Léon Blum's account of the affair (which I will discuss below) is that he emphasizes the degree to which, even for someone like himself who would later become a passionate partisan, this cause célèbre had been utterly forgotten by the time a small group of people took up the fight—Bernard Lazare, Lucien Herr, and Dreyfus's family. In the meantime Major Georges Picquart, the chief of the intelligence section and a member of the General Staff, had unmasked the actual author of the fateful *bordereau*, the real spy: Major Ferdinand Walsin Esterhazy, a singularly corrupt and unscrupulous figure. Picquart, however, was sworn to secrecy toward the public. His internal disclosure was countered by threats and forgeries from high-ranking members of the military, and Picquart was hastily transferred to Algeria. By then, however, the Dreyfusard opposition was gaining scope and momentum. Leading Dreyfusards were still counting on the government's willingness to investigate the case—a willingness that was not forthcoming, however. Esterhazy, at last openly accused of being the true spy, demanded military court proceedings to restore his honor; a trial followed, and he was acquitted in January 1898. But this devastating blow to Dreyfus's supporters was followed by Zola's famous article that compellingly argued for Dreyfus's innocence and pointed out the full corruption of the proceedings against him. It appeared in Clemenceau's *L'Aurore*; the spectacular title "J'accuse" was added by Clemenceau himself. The nation became more drastically and irreconcilably split, a schism that cut deep into families and long-standing cliques. There were pogroms in Algeria and the French provinces. Picquart was dismissed from the army and ultimately arrested for breach of secrecy. Zola was condemned to a year in prison for libel and fled to England when his appeal was dismissed. In July 1898, Cavaignac, the war minister of the newly elected government, presented the National Assembly with documents—forged by high-ranking members of the military—that were intended to prove Dreyfus's guilt. Radical right-wing organizations formed, planning a coup d'état. This was the nadir of the Dreyfus affair. But now the tables began to turn, albeit with tormenting slowness, via complex legal and political interventions and under growing pressure from the national and international public. The Waldeck-Rousseau government that had formed in June 1899 sought a compromise, a deal: a new trial in Rennes pronounced Dreyfus guilty once again, but found extenuating circumstances and reduced his sentence to ten years; several weeks later Dreyfus accepted this reprieve, which the radical faction of his supporters vehemently opposed. The convicted forger of the documents used against Dreyfus, Major Hubert-Joseph Henry, committed suicide in his cell with his own razor. The minister of war declared the incident "closed." When accepting his reprieve, however, Dreyfus had reserved the right to work toward restoring his reputation. Upon his return from Devil's Island, he applied for a retrial. In July 1906 the court of cassation reversed the verdict of Rennes and rehabilitated Dreyfus, who was reinstated in the military as a major the next day; the unbending Picquart returned to the army with the rank of a brigadier-general. Both circumstances were regarded as provocations by large intransigent factions of the military. A week later Dreyfus was named as a Chevalier of the Legion of Honor.

What later generations sketchily recalled as the triumph of a good cause actually stands as something profoundly ambivalent—truth was victorious, but its onward march was repeatedly interrupted by setbacks and was filled with grotesque episodes and unexpected obstacles, and in the end truth paid a very high price for its victory. Incidentally, as Léon Blum emphasizes, this victory was due in large part to Zola's great courage; his "J'accuse" appeared on January 13, 1898, at the very moment when Esterhazy's acquittal on January 11 had dashed all hopes of justice. The right never forgave Zola, and there have been ongoing speculations (never entirely lacking in plausibility) that Zola's death in 1902—he suffocated when a blocked chimney caused gases to build up in his bedroom—was not an accident and that the writer had fallen victim to a chauvinist plot.

The inconceivable barbarism of the Third Reich has led Europe to forget that, alongside Czarist Russia, France was the traditional home of anti-Semitism. The Dreyfus affair divided the nation in a way never seen before, or since. This is apparent over and over again in biographies from the time: Degas, a passionate admirer of the French army and among the staunchest of anti-Dreyfusards (along with Cézanne and Renoir), not only fell out with Monet and Pissarro, he turned his back on the Jewish Halévy family, whose famous salon had been his second home for years and whose members he had so often portrayed. (Incidentally, one of the most remarkable Degas portraits from the decades before the affair is the double portrait of the Belgian chief rabbi Elie-Aristide Astruc and the French general Émile Mellinet, who had worked side by side in the medical corps taking care of the sick during the siege of Paris, and had asked the painter for a "memorial to their brotherly efforts.") An epoch had come to an end.

The Dreyfus affair was an event with European, indeed global resonance. Chekhov and Mark Twain wrote about it. In the Swabian backwater of Hemmingen, Baroness Spitzemberg, the widow of Württemberg's envoy to Berlin, noted in her famous diary after Dreyfus's second conviction in 1899: "It is incredible how the question has whipped up feelings even in the lowest classes: often the farmers come to the post office late in the evening to pick up the local papers and read the news of the trial, rather than waiting to get them in the morning." The discussions in Germany and Austria were a complex subject unto themselves. The astonishing spectacle of Wilhelm Liebknecht, doyen of German social democracy, publishing a series of harsh anti-Dreyfusard articles in young Karl Kraus's journal *Die Fackel* can be put down to a mistrust of the liberal press and the fear that the German Reich might use the affair as an excuse to take a hard line toward a discredited France.

A little book published in 1935 still gives what may be the best sense of what the Dreyfus affair was and how it felt. It is called *Souvenirs sur l'affaire*, and its author is Léon Blum. Readers may know him as the great French statesman who succeeded Jean Jaurès as one of the leading figures of French socialism, a man whose name is now associated chiefly with the Popular Front governments between 1936 and 1938. The *front populaire* achieved several epochal social reforms, introducing such things as paid vacations. An elderly worker once wrote to Blum to thank him for the opportunity to see the sea once in his life.

After France was defeated during World War II, Blum openly opposed right-wing collaborationists and called on the socialists to respond with resistance; when the Vichy regime tried him in February 1942, he and his co-defendants pulled off such an impressive and elegant defense that the trial was ultimately called off—strikingly echoing the acquittal of the communist Dimitroff in the Reichstag fire trial. Blum's life was spared because he and several other prominent figures were kept as hostages until the end of the war to be used as security in the event of negotiations with the Allies.

Born in 1872, Blum experienced the Dreyfus affair as a young lawyer and writer; the drama seems to have played a crucial role in politicizing him, alongside his encounter with Jean Jaurès, which itself was closely bound up with the affair. One of the most fascinating features of his account is the description of the first weeks and months after the affair truly got underway, when it was unclear how the most prominent journalists and "intellectuals" would position themselves: Who would take Dreyfus's side, who would refuse their support, who would dither? The profound disappointments and pleasant surprises of these weeks made Blum conclude that in a genuine crisis people's reactions can never be predicted from their previous behavior. His account of the Dreyfus affair has the charm of a youthful memory, preserved still fresh in energetic, naïve immediacy, yet joined with the sad, dignified reflections of a man who has turned to skepticism. Though rigorous in their pursuit of truth, his *Souvenirs* are highly intimate, a fragment of an unwritten autobiography. He evokes the figures of his youth, his initiation into politics. The result is profoundly moving. In the year 1935, with Europe's greatest catastrophe looming, a politician and *homme de lettres* meditates on the great event of his youth, which for a time thrust all other questions into the background, even eclipsing everyday life for the committed champions of Dreyfus's innocence. Blum was prompted to set pen to paper by the death of Dreyfus that same year; long since rehabilitated, he had been readmitted to the army with full honors and served in World War I as a lieutenant colonel, commanding an artillery unit. But above and beyond the specific occasion, Blum was inspired by a profound disquiet. He immersed himself in his memories to delight in the freshness of his own youth and commemorate vanished comrades in arms. But the true, hidden endeavor implicit in this labor of memory was one that he clearly felt unable to master. To this day it seems an impossible endeavor: to find a convincing explanation for the hatred, intransigent and immune to reason and scruple, with which the right persecuted Dreyfus even after his innocence became evident. Blum powerfully depicts the Dreyfusards' incredulous astonishment, their stupefaction when, quite early on, they seemed to have reached their goal, convinced that now that the truth was on the table, the nation would allow its "lost son" a triumphant return from exile—and instead found themselves faced with a wall of cold resistance. Reflecting on the anti-Dreyfusards' boundless aggression,

Blum gingerly asked: "What drove them? What guided them? Even today, thirty-five years later, as I reflect on this past with mature, cool rationality, it seems to me that I still lack certain elements for a solution to this question." In 1935, this question was posed in the long shadow of the catastrophe whose distant overture the Dreyfus affair would prove to have been—with its dark menace, it posed once again the shabby, monstrous, manifest, and unfathomable riddle of nationalist furor and anti-Semitism. One shivers to read the first mention of the Dreyfus affair in the diaries of Harry Graf Kessler. The entry from January 28, 1898, records remarks made by the art historian Julius Meier-Graefe, including the following: that the Dreyfus affair was "a little practical lesson in political science expressly for the Jews."

"'You know…why they can't produce the proofs of Dreyfus's guilt. Apparently it's because he's the lover of the War Minister's wife, that's what people are saying on the sly.' 'Ah! I thought it was the Prime Minister's wife.'" A scrap of conversation, brimming with supercilious malice, from Marcel Proust's *In Search of Lost Time*—specifically, the long scene set at the salon of the Duchesse de Guermantes, where Dreyfus is the main topic of conversation. Readers of the *Recherche* are well aware that the affair plays a significant role in the novel, but the events made an even deeper impression on Proust than his monumental novel reveals. In Blum's book Proust appears for a moment in the procession of dedicated young people who met daily to plan ways of bringing about a retrial. The two had been classmates at the Lycée Condorcet; in her famous memoir, *Monsieur Proust*, Céleste Albaret recalls how he once spoke proudly of his class at school, many of whose members went on to achieve prominence—we were, he said, referring to Blum as well, "*une jolie petite troupe*." Elsewhere Céleste speaks of Proust's great admiration for the intelligence and warm heart of his boyhood friend.

Monsieur Proust also includes several passages about the Dreyfus affair. "'It was terrible,' he said. . . . 'Even Father was an anti-Dreyfusite, and we had a row. I didn't speak to him for a week.' He"—that is, Proust—"never told me what his mother, who was Jewish, thought. . . . It was just his humanity, his great love of truth." *C'était uniquement l'humanité, avec son grand amour de la verité.* She also writes: "You might have expected him to be timid, to be anxious to keep out of such conflicts, but he told me how he threw himself into the struggle and went to all the court hearings."

In fact, Proust performed an extremely important task for the Dreyfusards: he went to the reluctant Anatole France, whose fame as a writer lent great weight to his opinion, and ultimately persuaded him to sign the so-called "Manifesto of the Intellectuals," which appeared in *L'Aurore* the day after

Zola's "J'accuse." The epithet "Manifesto of the Intellectuals" was mockingly coined by one of Dreyfus's most emphatic detractors, Maurice Barrès; indeed, the very term "intellectual," so familiar to us, is a product of the polemics that swirled around the Dreyfus affair.

The colossal novel *In Search of Lost Time*, this "bafflingly rich and convoluted construct," as Adorno wrote in his appreciative "Short Commentaries on Proust," this *cathédrale inachevée*, as Proust himself called it, is famous for building incredibly long arcs of tension and development, ascendency and downfall, intimation and disclosure, clarification and new riddles, extending over thousands of pages, everything doubly reflected by the evocation of memory as the crucial arbiter of knowledge. Yet the details in *Recherche* have an irreducible significance. The novel sheds an ironic light on this focus on details as a caprice of the writer Bergotte; when he wants to praise a work, he always singles out a specific detail, usually an utterly marginal one. When the conversation turns to a certain book, he says: "There's a little girl in an orange shawl. It's excellent!" Or: "Oh yes, there's a passage in which there's a regiment marching along the street; yes, it's good!" This has great aesthetic plausibility— after all, what do we remember about novels in the end? At the same time, it is conceived as a comic detail itself. Yet once we have read the *Recherche*, we know that, in a serious turn of events, Bergotte will die at an art exhibition in front of Vermeer's famous painting *Gezicht op Delft*, swept away by his fascination with one tiny detail, the "little patch of yellow wall": "That's how I ought to have written," he thinks as he dies.

In the *Recherche*, Jewishness is both a structure and a telling detail. The novel has a great number of characters whose Jewish ancestry is a crucial trait, such as the banking family Israël, and two central characters are chiefly characterized through their Jewishness: indirectly Swann, the most important character alongside the narrator and the enigmatically desirable Albertine, and directly Bloch. Bloch is the most interesting character in this context, and he may be the one for whom the narrator secretly harbors the most affection (though he admires Swann as a role model). Bloch is gauche and forward, he has passionate views, he tries to do everything especially well, he provokes, he loves music, he gets on people's nerves. His first appearance as the narrator's friend, still a schoolboy here, almost at the beginning of "Combray," is marked by a vignette that thematizes Jewishness for the first time in the novel. Due to his eccentric behavior, "Bloch was not invited to the house again."

At first he had been well received there. It is true that my grandfather made out that, whenever I formed a strong attachment to any one of my friends and brought him home with me, that friend was invariably a Jew; to which he would not have objected on principle—indeed his own friend Swann was of Jewish extraction—had he not found that the Jews whom I chose as friends were not usually of the best type. And so whenever I brought a new friend home my grandfather seldom failed to start humming the "O, God of our fathers" from *La Juive*, or else "Israel, break thy chains," singing the tune alone, of course, to an "um-ti-tum-ti-tum, tra-la"; but I used to be afraid that my friend would recognize it and be able to reconstruct the words.

Before seeing them, merely on hearing their names, about which, as often as not, there was nothing particularly Hebraic, he would divine not only the Jewish origin of such of my friends as might indeed be Jewish, but even at times some skeleton in their family cupboard.

"And what's the name of this friend of yours who is coming this evening?"

"Dumont, grandpapa."

"Dumont! Oh, I don't like the sound of that."

And he would sing:

Archers, be on your guard!
Watch without rest, without sound.

And then, after a few adroit questions on points of detail, he would call out "On guard! on guard," or, if it were the victim himself who had already arrived, and had been unwittingly obliged, by subtle interrogation, to admit his origins, then my grandfather, to show us that he had no longer any doubts, would merely look at us, humming under his breath the air of

What! do you hither guide the feet
Of this timid Israelite?

(The little leitmotif of what one might call old-fashioned jovial anti-Semitism makes it clear, in passing, why someone like Bloch would have a brusque and clumsy manner.)

In a famous scene, comical, yet somehow also moving in its depiction of a minor humiliation, Bloch commits a faux pas at the salon of the Marquise de Villeparisis.

Bloch rose, and in his turn came over to look at the flowers which Mme de Villeparisis was painting.... [He] wanted to express his admiration in an appropriate gesture, but only succeeded in knocking over the glass containing the spray of apple blossom with his elbow, and all the water was spilled on the carpet.

"You really have a fairy's touch," the historian said to the Marquise; having his back turned to me at that moment, he had not noticed Bloch's clumsiness.

But Bloch took the remark as a jibe at him, and to cover his shame with a piece of insolence, retorted: "It's not of the slightest importance; I'm not wet."

Shame, and the brashness that attempts to disguise shame. . . . On the beach of the now-fashionable spa town of Balbec, the narrator and his friend Saint-Loup hear, in passing, a loud voice from inside a tent ranting against the "swarm of Jews" that has descended upon Balbec in the tone of the most vulgar anti-Semitism and using classic anti-Semitic phrases ("I am not in principle irremediably hostile to the Jewish race, but here there is a plethora of them.") "The man," we then learn, "who thus inveighed against Israel emerged at last from the tent, and we raised our eyes to behold this anti-Semite. It was my old friend Bloch." Bloch, a passionate Dreyfusard, avidly follows, like the author himself, all the affair's court proceedings. Proust writes:

. . . he would come away so enamoured of everything that had happened in court that when he returned home in the evening he longed to immerse himself again in the thrilling drama and would hurry out to a restaurant frequented by both parties in search of friends with whom he would go over the day's proceedings interminably and make up, by a supper ordered in an imperious tone which gave him the illusion of power, for the hunger and exhaustion of a day begun so early and unbroken by any interval for lunch.

I wish to add only that the anti-Semitic hatred to which Charlus subjects Bloch seems to be nourished by a vague infatuation.

The Dreyfus affair has a wealth of consequences in the *Recherche*. Odette climbs the social ladder by organizing an anti-Dreyfusard salon. The foolish Duc de Guermantes is very much against Dreyfus until a chance encounter with "three clever ladies" turns him into a resolute Dreyfusard. Dreyfus's most energetic supporter, next to Bloch, is the opportunistic, part ludicrous, part sinister Madame Verdurin, who carefully uses her partisan stance to strategically expand her influence and thus her salon.

At one point the narrator of the *Recherche* says of himself: "I who have just fought several duels unafraid on account of the Dreyfus case . . ." This sounds very *engagé*, but in keeping with Proust's characteristic techniques, the narrator mentions this duel only in the context of his notorious fear of fresh, cold air—to which he dared expose himself back in the day of his early morning duels. This recalls a remark Proust made about the only duel which he himself fought. It was a pistol duel (neither of the combatants was a swordsman) with the literary dandy Jean Lorrain, who had written an insolent and personally insulting review of Proust's first book, *Les plaisirs et les jours*. Proust supposedly claimed that the only thing that frightened him about the duel was the thought of failing to show up punctually for an appointment so early in the morning.

These are trivial ironies. But Proust's treatment of the Dreyfus affair in the *Recherche* follows this ironic principle to such a degree that it reveals the higher truth in the work of art—and a conscious practice on the part of the author. From a naïve point of view, nothing would have been more obvious than for Proust, the passionate Dreyfusard, to devise the roles in his novel in such a way that the characters' partisan stance for or against Dreyfus would show the degree of sympathy they are supposed to enjoy. But here the words of Karl Kraus hold par excellence: "It doesn't matter whether an opinion is correct, it always matters who holds it." One might add that no single sentence of the *Recherche* reveals a truth that can be isolated; everything is true only in its context, and these contexts are extremely complex. All the same, there is perhaps no concept that Proust treats with more dignity than that of the truth. His irony is not an isolated device, it is an instrument for depicting the dialectic of the universal (the ethical truth) and the particular (human life and *its* truth).

The invocation of a very particular fate that combines consciousness of ineluctable uniqueness with a commitment to universal values such as truth and justice often appears as a signature of Jewishness in the modern era, and repeatedly as the self-definition of Jewish thinkers in the Enlightenment; the defense of these universal truths appears as the special mission of a Judaism that insists, all the same, on adhering to its exceptionalism. The calm refusal to convert to Christianity, as affirmed by Moses Mendelssohn with great dignity in the face of Lavater's agitated impertinence, upholds both the particular and the commitment to the universal truths of the Enlightenment.

In this Jewishness, which is committed equally to the truth of the universal and the particular, one glimpses for a moment a signature of modern literature. That sounds like a very sweeping claim, but I invite you to think about it for a moment. There is a general consensus that, undeniably, the three most important canonical writers of world literature in the first half of the twentieth century are Proust, Joyce, and Kafka (the jury is still out on the second half).

Incidentally, these three canonical *chefs d'oeuvre* of modernism—if I might change the pace with a digression—are linked by a peculiar affinity to half-sleep, to the zone between dream and waking that is marked simultaneously by the perturbation of longing and nightmares and by a nervous over-alertness. One need only think of the *Recherche*, a colossal work launched by a hallucinatory first sentence: "For a long time I would go to bed early." These early bedtimes of childhood, this waiting for mother and sleep, this concentrated reflection on the day that has passed, and this eavesdropping on the world of the adults, corresponds to a passage at the end of *Ulysses*, the endless-seeming inner monologue of Molly Bloom as she lies in bed, half awake and half dreaming, the stream of consciousness of the unfaithful Penelope, the mother goddess, humanity in half-sleep (a half-sleep that will plunge to immense depths in *Finnegans Wake*). And it would be easy to compile a Kafka anthology with passages like the one that begins *The Metamorphosis*: "When Gregor Samsa woke one morning from troubled dreams, he found himself transformed right there in his bed into some sort of monstrous insect." This collection would contain the "Country Doctor's" bedside visit, where he himself is laid in the sick man's bed while the village school's choir sing "an utterly simple tune" with the words: "Strip his clothes off, then he'll heal us, if he doesn't, kill him dead! Only a doctor, only a doctor." The arc extends to "The Judgment," in which the son brings his father to bed and, just before the old man rises up to pass the death sentence on his son, we hear the beautiful, uncanny words: "Am I well covered-up?" And all this would cast a special light on the beginning of *The Trial*, where the words "Someone must have slandered Josef K." open the morning scene in which K., "from his pillow," is gazing into a window across the way when a stranger steps into his room. "'Who are you?' asked K., and immediately sat halfway up in bed."

This little digression is intended less to demonstrate that surprising connections can be drawn between disparate works than to recall that this ubiquitous half-sleep lies precisely between the radical individuality of the dream and the universally binding nature of waking reality. At first glance, the Jewishness that links these canonic writers also seems to have disparate traits. In Kafka's work the strong impression of Jewishness is undeniable, yet it is difficult to pin down. Though Kafka scholarship has long since moved past the postwar stage in which the author's work was supposed to represent one great allegory of Judaism, no one would deny that Kafka is emphatically to be regarded as a Jewish author. And Joyce? Well, the hero of his magnum opus is a Jew, of course; the Odysseus of the world-spanning Dublin day in *Ulysses* is a little ad man by the name of Leopold

Bloom. On Bloomsday in 1984, Wolfgang Hildesheimer gave a beautiful speech in his honor: "The Jewishness of Mr. Bloom." The book does begin with a reincarnation of the autobiographical protagonist from *Portrait of the Artist as a Young Man*, Stephen Dedalus, but this Irish-Catholic-anti-Catholic stand-in for the author is relegated to the role of Telemachus.

In the case of Proust, the question about the "Jewishness" of the work is provocative. He loved his mother above all else; in the *Recherche* he gave Jewishness a structural function that rendered it as one of the great tormented, productive, mysteriously fascinating manifestations of the outsider, like homosexuality and like artistic inspiration. But wasn't he actually a Christian? Isn't the term that he himself used for the *Recherche*—an uncompleted cathedral—more than an architectural fantasy, rather something approaching a confession of faith? It is an extremely difficult question. It is probably impossible to definitively determine whether Proust's aesthetics lean toward religious forms merely due to the magic of tradition and—despite all his sardonic skepticism about society—to his profound respect for cultural heritage. How to interpret Proust's letter to Jacques Rivière from February 1914, in which he refers to his novel as a "dogmatic work" in the service of "TRUTH"? What does it mean when the author, facing death, writes to the pious poet

Francis Jammes and asks him to pray to Saint Joseph to ease his dying? Is it evidence of his own profound piety, is it an additional indication of Proust's great, affectionate courtesy toward his friends, is it a humble metaphor? Proust asked for a rosary to be placed in his hands on his deathbed— though Céleste Albaret forgot it in the end. However, it was a very specific rosary, an object of memory, saturated with friendship, a present from the sarcastic Lucie Faure. What did this object mean to him? What is the meaning of the churches that the narrator loves so deeply in the *Recherche*? When the steeple of Saint-Hilaire looms on the horizon as a delicate line, it is as though a fingernail had scratched it in the sky because the painter was "anxious to give to such a landscape, to so pure a piece of nature, this little sign of art, this single indication of human existence." Art and human existence appear as the truly meaningful forms of religion.

When the *Recherche* is juxtaposed with the actual experience of the Dreyfus affair, the artistic insistence on the mystery of individual existence might seem like a retreat from the moral imperative of public political commitment. But we do well to trust to Proust's logic, the higher "commitment." Faithfulness to universal values is expressed in a radical loyalty to the unfathomable uniqueness of the individual human being.

During the affair, Maurice Barrès accused the Dreyfusards of being infatuated by abstractions such as truth and justice. "The Dreyfus affair is an orgy of metaphysicians. They judge everything abstractly. We judge everything with respect to France." We live in a time in which the automatic appeal to the interests of a nation—its security, its stature, its sphere of influence—makes international law irrelevant. (Here, incidentally, it would be worth repeating Hegel's question "Who thinks abstractly?") To me it seems indisputable that modern literature, especially Proust, contains an ongoing covert discourse about the dialectic of the universal and the particular. Proust's art fuses them together. The fact that there is no simple resolution to this dialectic, and that the much-admired Swann turns out to be extremely naïve in his increasing inability to judge things except with relation to the Dreyfus affair, is a skeptical conclusion, but its particularity, in turn, lies in its passionateness.

The original format of this piece has been largely maintained; it was a talk given at an event at the Simon Dubnow Institute for Jewish History and Culture at the University of Leipzig, marking the departure of Professor Dan Diner, its founding director. It was based on two older essays: the preface to my translation of Léon Blum's Souvenirs sur l'affaire (Beschwörung der Schatten) *(Berlin: Berenberg, 2005), and my review of Anita Albus's exploration of Proust's work,* Im Licht der Finsternis (*Frankfurter Allgemeine Zeitung, 2011*).

Two Gastronomic Vignettes from the Nineteenth Century

THERE IS A certain tradition in French cuisine with a paradoxical connection to French history: following the revolution, bourgeois cuisine saw itself as a sort of heir to court cuisine, and on formal occasions the elaborate productions of the aristocratic table were perpetuated in upper-middle-class dining rooms. This can be observed in many different details, for instance in the history of the table centerpiece. Among the oddest imitations of aristocratic dining extravagances, utterly lost to us today, was the custom of serving edible *structures*. The only example we are still familiar with (at least from shop windows) is the wedding cake, which combines elements of architecture, sculpture, and occasionally portrait painting.

Surprisingly, Balzac, the great diner, never provides a

136

detailed description of a grand dinner with all its accessories,
a lack of interest implying a certain critique of the stultifying
pomposity of these elaborate rituals—he is more concerned
with depicting *en detail* the dreariness of the dinner table
at Pension Vauquer. But in one superficially unremarkable
passage, the bourgeois novel at its peak casually pulls off a
radical exposure of the custom of *staging* food.

A country wedding is being celebrated. The tables have
been set up in the open air. First the author describes the
meal, lavish yet simple, down-to-earth yet festive. And it
comes to a special culmination and climax:

A confectioner of Yvetot had been entrusted with the
tarts and sweets. As he had only just set up in the place,
he had taken a lot of trouble, and at dessert he himself
brought in a set dish [*une pièce montée*] that evoked loud
cries of wonderment. To begin with, at its base there was
a square of blue cardboard, representing a temple with
porticoes, colonnades, and stucco statuettes all round,
and in the niches constellations of gilt paper stars; then
on the second stage was a castle of Savoy cake, surrounded
by many fortifications in candied angelica, almonds, rai-
sins, and quarters of oranges; and finally, on the upper
platform a green field with rocks set in lakes of jam, nut-
shell boats, and a small Cupid balancing himself in a

chocolate swing whose two uprights ended in real rose-buds at the top.

Until night they ate. When any of them were too tired of sitting, they went out for a stroll in the yard, or for a game of *bouchon* in the granary, and then returned to table.

The description of the cake served at Emma Bovary's wedding is embedded in the unfolding of a rustic celebration at which guests doggedly eat vast quantities and devote themselves to coarse pleasures, lifting weights and grabbing women—boorish larks whose ingenuous foolishness is immune to accusations of bad taste. In this rural, archaic milieu, the cake is a foreign body greeted with cries of astonishment: an exotic spectacle. The ambitious confectioner delivers it from Yvetot, a provincial Norman town on the road from Tostes (the scene of the action) to Le Havre, much smaller than the almost equidistant Rouen. And yet it is "modern" and unexpected: its appearance marks the incursion of urban luxury into the rural backwater. Within the context of the novel, it is an artfully subtle symbol. The kitschy details of this confectionary construction discreetly reflect the bride's perishable sentimentality, her "Bovarysme." "The lake of jam," Nabokov writes in his brilliant analysis (*Lectures on Literature*), "is a kind of premonitory emblem of the romantic Swiss lakes upon which, to the sound of Lamartine's fashionable lyrical verse, Emma Bovary, the budding adulteress, will drift in her dreams; and we shall meet again the little cupid on the bronze clock in the squalid splendor of the Rouen hotel room where Emma has her assignations with Léon, her second lover."

This cake's symbolic role within Flaubert's novel is one thing; one can also seek to decode its gastronomic history. It is no mere pastry, it is a structure with mimetic pretensions. Such efforts to shape and reshape are familiar even from the literature of antiquity: the *locus classicus* is the grotesquely elaborate, endless, tasteless feast held by the nouveau riche Trimalchio in Petronius's *Satyricon*, the only Latin novel of imperial Rome that has (in fragmentary form) survived. Here the dishes nearly always seek to simulate something else, shaped from a different substance than anticipated or imitating something they are not—"quinces with thorns stuck in them to resemble sea urchins." Of the chef—known as Daedalus for his virtuosity—it is claimed: "Just say the word, and he'll whip you up a fish out of sowbelly, pigeons out of bacon, doves from ham and chicken from pigs' knuckles." Another possibility presented here is to make foodstuffs (or other physical materials) into riddles:

prizes are raffled off, and the person who wins a moray (*muraena*) is given a mouse tied to a frog (*mus/rana*). The author, skewering the aesthetic strategies at Nero's court as people seek to outdo and astonish one another, portrays these corny puns as examples of nouveau riche tastelessness. But they also reflect a naive, childlike pleasure in the transformation of material, in eating something so skillfully imitative that for a moment one is able to fall for the illusion. All the endless jests of Trimalchio's banquet aim to astonish: in staged scenes, cooks and servants perform mini-dramas of deception, seeking to arouse both amazement and disgust. The decisive factor is always the surprise effect. For instance, the simplest variant, a mere effigy, is represented by a statue of Priapus made from cake.

There is something embarrassingly pretentious about these arts. This emerges even more clearly when we encounter them once again—first in a simplified form, then gradually becoming more and more luxurious, though still relatively coarse—on the dining tables of the medieval and early modern courts. The dishes are full of ostentation, just as they are often systematically over-seasoned, too sweet and spicy, to demonstrate that the hosts can afford expensive spices; they abound in crude surprise effects, just as guests taking their seats at a princely table might be suddenly drenched by hidden fountain jets. Those things gradually vanish from the dining table, those animals painstakingly restored to their original shape, those sculptures of lard, of ice cream, of mashed potatoes, those castles and parks confected from sugar. Regarding the latter, the late, already anachronistic apotheosis of confectionary architecture comes in the treatise *Le pâtissier pittoresque*, written by a great chef whose name paradoxically evokes a fast: Marie-Antoine Carême, "le Palladio de la cuisine," Talleyrand's cook at the Congress of Vienna. Published in 1815, his book puts all of them on parade once more, the *"grand pavillon gothique à 44 colonnes"* and the *"grand cabinet chinois,"* the antique and picturesque structures of pastry and fondant. Our era has forgotten them. In middle-class cuisine the transformation of food into structures has dwindled away, taught by old cookbooks only for extremely rare occasions, so that now the art has vanished almost entirely; nothing remains of the great edifices and the "pieces montées" but the little paper flags and Japanese parasols stuck into desserts. One last, almost parodic echo is found on the children's menus of German ice-cream parlors, featuring effigies of Mickey Mouse and other cartoon characters, imitations of spaghetti or fried eggs. This goes back to the confectionary tradition—candy in different shapes, chocolate cigars, fondant Easter Bunnies. Naturally the wedding cake, as one gigantic sweet, is part of this confectionary practice, but while the sculptures produced by chocolatiers and candy factories generally serve as gifts, standalone items isolated from the meal, the cake is served up and displayed on the dinner table. Thus it stands as the final monument to the epoch that sought to mold the courses of a formal feast into astonishing shapes.

Cake is predestined for architecture by the malleability of its material—but this childishly pleasurable plasticity also gives cakes an odd affinity to comedy; the cake fight is a topos of old slapstick movies. Two Laurel and Hardy films stake out the possibilities: *From Soup to Nuts* (1928, MGM/ Hal Roach) is an étude, of some interest for the history of the upper-middle-class society dinner, in which Stan and Ollie are hired as servants and Ollie, in balletically choreographed variations, keeps falling face-down onto the cake he is trying to serve. *The Battle of the Century* (1927, MGM/ Hal Roach) begins with a slip on the traditional banana peel and brings in a pastry shop's delivery truck to build, step by step, an escalation of misunderstandings and universal retaliatory urges that fills an entire street, ultimately shown in one wide-angle shot, with a rampaging crowd of people throwing pies at each other and covering vehicles and passersby in whipped cream. These are the iron laws of slapstick cinema: a banana is for slipping on; a cake is for throwing in someone's face. Cake has something inherently comical about it. But in the mythology of the cinema it also acquires something slightly sinister; the more common it becomes, on festive occasions, to have a girl jump out of an outsized cake, striking an innocently lascivious pose to the delight of the guest of honor, the more likely it seems that the cake might bring forth quite a different, lethal surprise—the fate of "Spats" Colombo at the meeting of the Friends of Italian Opera in *Some Like It Hot*. In *Singin' in the Rain* the cake's two functions are elegantly synthesized: first Debbie Reynolds jumps out of the cake in a professional capacity, and a moment later, in private rage, she is throwing its icing at Gene Kelly (hitting Jean Hagen). The wedding cake is, as it were, the gift of fortune from which the (hopefully attractive) future shall emerge.

The cake served in *Madame Bovary* is a seemingly incidental detail which the author presents as though it were merely an interesting facet of the sociology of taste, part of realism's program of offering a thick description of a society's customs. But it is more than that. Nabokov, that magnificent reader, recognized with his unerring gaze that the multi-level, many-faceted wedding cake picks up another motif of the novel, one that appears at the very beginning. It sounds improbable, yet once you have seen it, it is utterly clear and evident:

the motif is the cap worn by the adolescent Charles Bovary as he enters the room where "we were in class" in the first line of the first chapter. This cap is a grotesque object, one of those things "whose dumb ugliness has depths of expression, like an imbecile's face." What contributes most to its ugliness is its composite character; it is a preposterous assemblage containing "traces of the bearskin, shake, billycock hat, sealskin cap, and cotton nightcap." The uppermost part of the elaborately ugly structure is made of cardboard; Nabokov notes that the cake, with its cardboard base, starts where the cap leaves off. Both, in Nabokov's words, are "a pathetic affair in poor taste." The cap and the cake embody the sort of tastelessness that has something sad, helpless, almost touching about it. The novel is constructed to make them mirror each other in a meticulous arrangement—both of them symbols of failed effort.

In a period which, as the novel was written, was beginning to call itself the "age of reason," this attempt to salvage some vestige of theatricality from a feudal cuisine of surprise and spectacle is a gastronomical flop. It is a flop not only in Flaubert's merciless eyes: even his contemporary readers had to realize that despite the naive provincial audience's cries of amazement the cake is an embarrassment. (The cries demonstrate that the guests are still in a state of consumerist innocence.) Yet in this object Flaubert lets ugliness come into its own. No author dissected the age's supposed reason and revealed its vanity with such sardonic precision. Conversely, at times his novels reveal a great, humble respect for what is despised. Of course an object such as the wedding cake, that last veteran of the edible edifices, is nothing more now than a melancholy testimonial to tastelessness. But there is something touching about its ugliness: part of Flaubert's greatness is his ability to depict the cake simultaneously as a monstrosity and as an affecting attempt to create a thing of beauty with grotesquely unfit means.

AN UNCOMPROMISINGLY BRITISH MEAL

THE YEAR 1889 saw the publication of *The Wrong Box*, one of the three novels on which Robert Louis Stevenson collaborated with his stepson Lloyd Osbourne, whose share in these fictions should not be underestimated. It is a grotesque criminal comedy in which various law-abiding citizens unexpectedly find a corpse on their hands; as in "The Hunchback's Tale" from *1001 Nights*, they attempt to unobtrusively pass on the mysterious, sinister object. In the course of the ingeniously labyrinthine plot, a young man of good family is forced to make his way to London, penniless and on foot, from a rural backwater; exhausted and scruffy he arrives home (John Street in Bloomsbury) late at night, berates his brother, whose intrigues put him in this plight, and cries for dinner. There is nothing in the house. The starving man rages: "You nincompoop!... Ain't we house-holders? Don't they know us at that hotel where Uncle Parker used to come? Be off with you; and if you ain't back in half an hour, and if the dinner ain't good...." The hotel obliges, and soon we see the meal that we shall now take a moment to examine: the sort of meal, that is, that an upper-middle-class hotel would send to this sort of private house-hold in London around 1890 (in a contemporary novel, strictly speaking, but by all indications it is a realistic portrayal).

The room looked comparatively habitable by the time the dinner came; and the dinner itself was good: strong gravy soup, fillets of sole, mutton chops and tomato sauce, roast beef done rare with roast potatoes, cabinet pudding, a piece of Chester cheese, and some early celery: a meal uncompromisingly British, but supporting.

"Thank God!" said John, his nostrils sniffing wide, surprised by joy into the unwonted formality of grace.

146

This menu includes a dish that is almost completely unknown today. The mutton chops and tomato sauce, which sound exotic today even to British diners, must once have been one of England's most commonplace dishes. There is a nice piece of literary evidence for its ubiquity. In chapter 34 of Dickens's sublime first novel, *The Pickwick Papers* (1836–1837), the eponymous hero is put on trial. To his outraged astonishment, his landlady has sued him for supposedly breaching his promise to marry her. The Bardell vs. Pickwick case—perhaps the most famous court proceedings in English literature next to the trial of the Knave of Hearts in *Alice in Wonderland*, twenty-eight years later—is extremely comical; this comedy, which actually lands Pickwick in jail at first, is lent an unsettling edge by the total unscrupulousness of the opposing lawyers and the effectiveness of their absurd rhetoric. The notes which Pickwick has written his landlady, consisting of utterly innocent banalities, are now read out in court by Mrs. Bardell's lawyer with grand forensic gestures as though they were secret erotic messages, including the following: "Dear Mrs. B.—Chops and Tomato sauce. Yours, Pickwick." While the lawyer sees this as monstrous evidence of Don Juanism—"Gentlemen, what does this mean? 'Chops and Tomato sauce. Yours, Pickwick!' Chops! Gracious heavens! and Tomato sauce! Gentlemen, is the happiness of a sensitive and confiding female to be trifled away by such shallow artifices as these?"—the tiny missive is evidence for us (and present-day British readers and diners) that this must be a completely ordinary dish.

But the chops and tomato sauce are not merely a fine example for the vagaries of fashion that sweep away once-classic styles of food preparation: nowadays mutton itself, next to beef the most important meat in early modern England (as even Pepys's diary shows), has long since lost its significance in English cuisine. Except in Indian cooking, its consumption has dropped considerably; lamb, imported in large quantities from New Zealand, may have supplanted the tougher, stronger-flavored mutton. Mutton is still found, but in the cities it is served mainly "in some archly retro kitchens," as a friend wrote to me disapprovingly.

What strikes us today—apart from the massive, stolid, copious character of the meal, which the authors themselves emphasize and which, of course, is partly explained by John's ravenous appetite following his deliverance from vagabondage—is the absence of vegetables. This reflects the impression that travelers have always had of England. Here vegetables appear only in a "marginalized" form—pushed aside into the tomato sauce. And in the form of celery. The celery poses something of a riddle. As it comes after the cheese in the list of courses, one might assume that it is served raw. But that is not certain, and a remark made by John—"there's been a strong frost these two last nights, and I can't get it out of my bones; the celery will be just the ticket"—implies something served warm. Either way, it is not celery root, but celery stalks, which even today have such significance in England and the United States that in comics they are often seen protruding from the top of the grocery bag as it is carried from the supermarket to the car, a symbol of *grocery shopping* per se.

The soup is not a clear broth, but a "gravy soup" thickened with flour and vegetables (nothing special—"And I thought I didn't like gravy soup!" the hungry John exclaims). The fish is Dover sole, *solea solea*, more or less the classic English fish served at the time. The dessert, "cabinet pudding," is a bread pudding made with white bread, amaretto biscuits, or ladyfingers with dried or candied fruits. The name, with its political ring, is cryptic, but long attested, with parallel names such as *"pouding à la chancelière."* The crucial thing is that the English "pudding" has nothing whatsoever to do with our usage of the word (denoting what is usually a cheap, synthetic, gelatinous children's dessert). First and foremost, "pudding" simply describes dessert as such ("What's for pudding?"); in a stricter sense, the word refers to steamed dishes such as cabinet pudding or the famous plum pudding.

And so we have a soup, then fish, two meat courses—
mutton with tomato sauce and beef with potatoes (peeled,
halved or quartered, and roasted)—a massive dessert, and
cheese and celery. Another striking detail is the almost
aggressively British habit of serving meat and fish without
sauce, sauce being characteristic of French cuisine. In this
context, the tomato sauce is a fine example of an "Other"
that is adapted to native customs and no longer experienced
as alien. Otherwise there is nothing that is not native; even
the cheese is British, and rather banal, not Stilton, not even
cheddar. "Uncompromisingly British"—the authors' phrase
picks up a motif that secretly centers on the roast beef
(which, to boot, is served rare, i.e. "English"). We see in
Hogarth's painting *The Gate of Calais—Oh, the Roastbeef
of Old England* (1748) how this cut of meat became a national
mythos. In the painting, gaunt French soldiers—and what
looks like a Highland Scot who fled to France following the
failed Jacobin rebellion of 1745—stare longingly at a massive
piece of imported beef as it is lugged past by a cook. French
tyranny and poverty is juxtaposed with British freedom and
well-being (*beef and liberty!*). It was not for nothing that
Hogarth belonged to a patriotic club called "The Sublime
Society of Beefsteaks"—one of the rare instances of members of a particular nation naming themselves after a characteristic dish; usually, as we know, this is done pejoratively

by outsiders (garlic-eaters, frogs, etc.—indeed, the French used to call the English *les rosbifs*). Incidentally, "French cuisine" as the dream and nightmare of the English imagination constitutes a whole chapter unto itself; the English cultivated fears of its decorative luxury and artificiality. I shall merely quote a brief, rather tipsy conversation from Kingsley Amis's novel *Take a Girl Like You* (1960):—"I don't really mind where we go. As long as I haven't got to have any of that foreign muck with all fat and things, and sauces."—"That's right."—"I can't see why they have to mess about with decent food."—"Spoils it, doesn't it?"—"They just mess it up."—"Covering it with all those sauces and muck."—"You don't know what you're eating any more."— "All you can taste is the sauce and muck."—"It all tastes the same."

What does John drink with his meal? He brusquely sends his brother to the cellar for "fizz" (champagne) and port. It is difficult to say whether this reflects John's recklessly sybaritic mood in his state of extremis, or whether these are the beverages that would have normally accompanied a meal like the one described. Perhaps we can leave the last word to one of the correspondents I sounded out regarding this little passage: "I'm not too sure, but the Brits will drink anything in any combination as long as it contains alcohol."

Gaslight, Fog, Jack the Ripper

[D]o you like the mingled gas and orange odours of the theatre, do you like the sound of the orchestra tuning, the sight of the footlights suddenly lightening...?

—ARTHUR MACHEN, *Far Off Things*

THE CURRENT debate about Berlin's last remaining gas lanterns revealed—who would have thought it?—that gas lighting has not yet been entirely eliminated from our cities. As with many things we take for granted, a chance circumstance can open up a chink into the past. To walk at night through brightly or at least partially lit streets is quite a late achievement of urban civilization. Under Napoleon, Cologne's clergy supposedly resisted the introduction of municipal street lighting because it disrupted the world's ordained order, the alternation between light and dark—the objection may strike us as ludicrous, but it holds, if not a kernel of truth, at least a powerful reminder. Thirty years ago Wolfgang Schivelbusch, in his masterful study *Licht-blicke. Zur Geschichte der künstlichen Helligkeit im 19.*

Jahrhundert (Glimmers of Light: The History of Artificial Illumination in the Nineteenth Century) traced the slow, halting technical and administrative process by which regular street lighting was introduced. In the nineteenth century gas lighting superseded torches and oil lamps, and though later it was largely replaced by electricity, it survived for quite some time in sophisticated forms such as Auer's gas mantle. What we shall glance at here is not the chronicle of technological innovation, charming as it is—the gaslight dispenses with the wick, electricity dispenses with the flame—but the mythology of gaslit streets and houses as enshrined in books and films, the special luminosity of an auratic historical memory.

The familiar, "proper" form of gas street lighting is the lantern on a metal pole (one of those everyday objects that for generations were second nature, taken for granted until at last, like the telephone booth, they vanished but for a few nostalgic examples). A little meditation on the stalwart ugliness of the cast-iron street lantern is found in the work of G. K. Chesterton. At the beginning of the novel *The Man Who Was Thursday*, two poets, Syme and Gregory, get into a philosophical argument at an evening garden party. Finally Syme steps out into the street. "Directly outside the door stood a street lamp, whose gleam gilded the leaves of the tree that bent out over the fence behind him." Next to the lamp he spots Gregory, who asks with icy politeness for a moment's conversation. What about? "Gregory struck out with his stick at the lamp-post, and then at the tree. 'About this and this,' he cried; 'about order and anarchy. There is your precious order, that lean, iron lamp, ugly and barren; and there is anarchy, rich, living, reproducing itself—there is anarchy, splendid in green and gold.' 'All the same,' replied Syme patiently, 'just at present you only see the tree by the light of the lamp. I wonder when you would ever see the lamp by the light of the tree.'" The juxtaposition of the lamp and tree must have been an inspiration for Chesterton, for it recurs in one of the Father Brown stories, "The God of the Gongs," in the second collection *The Wisdom of Father Brown*. That story begins with the description of a gloomy winter day and "the flat Essex coast, where the monotony was the more inhuman for being broken at very long intervals by a lamp-post that looked less civilized than a tree, or a tree that looked more ugly than a lamp-post."

In Walter Benjamin's description of the bourgeois apartments of "the 1860s to the 1890s," which includes the famous words "On this sofa the aunt cannot but be murdered," the gentle, insistent sound of the gas lighting is the detail concluding the description of the interior "with its gigantic sideboards distended with carvings, the sunless corners where palms stand, the balcony embattled behind its balus-

trade, and the long corridors with their singing gas flames..."
All the same, the word "gas flame" today is more likely to
evoke city streets, especially the streets of Victorian London.
"I was at a house near Regent's Park last night, and when
I came away the fancy took me to walk home instead of
taking a hansom. It was a clear pleasant night enough, and
after a few minutes I had the streets pretty much to myself.
It's a curious thing, Austin, to be alone in London at night,
the gas-lamps stretching away in perspective, and the dead
silence, and then perhaps the rush and clatter of a hansom
on the stones, and the fire starting up under the horse's
hoofs." (Arthur Machen, *The Great God Pan*, 1894) In passages such as these, gas lighting becomes the signature of an
era—or rather a cipher of our mythical remembrance of a
historical period. For us, the primary quality distinguishing
the nineteenth century (a century that takes on an especially
auratic form toward its end, in the era embodied by Sherlock
Holmes and Jack the Ripper), is a great, cozy sense of security
brought out all the more vividly by the evocation of the
uncanny.

On a memorable morning of early December London opened its eyes
on a frigid gray mist.... From Bow even unto Hammersmith there
draggled a dull, wretched vapor, like the wraith of an impecunious
suicide come into a fortune immediately after the fatal deed."
—ISRAEL ZANGWILL, *The Big Bow Mystery* (1891)

In our mythology the natural environment of gaslight is fog
(just as neon calls for rain—Franz Josef Degenhardt: "It
rained in neon colors...").

In Dickens's novel *Bleak House*, the fog in the London
streets—embodying the logic of the all-enveloping, all-
obliterating court proceedings at the story's heart—serves
as a symbol of suffocating stagnation. We are so used to this
fog as the theatrical backdrop of mystery novels and detective movies that it is worth reminding ourselves how staggering London's fog actually seemed at the time, until shortly
after World War II the sky began to clear up thanks to fuel
regulations and technological advances. On the other hand,
the most practical place to look for this historical remembrance is in detective stories.

"In the Fog" is the title of an ingenious mystery story—
actually a brief cycle of stories with a framing device—by
Richard Harding Davis published in three installments in
1902 in *Windsor Magazine*. It leads the reader deep into the
fog indeed. One of the narrators has dinner at a friend's;

preparing to leave, he hears the servant whistle long and hard for a hansom cab with no result. Nothing comes. Are the cab men on strike? No—his friend is now standing at the window—"'You have never seen a London fog, have you?' he asked. 'Well, come here. This is one of the best, or, rather, one of the worst, of them.' I joined him at the window, but I could see nothing. Had I not known that the house looked out upon the street I would have believed that I was facing a dead wall. I raised the sash and stretched out my head, but still I could see nothing. Even the light of the street lamps opposite, and in the upper windows of the barracks, had been smothered in the yellow mist. The lights of the room in which I stood penetrated the fog only to the distance of a few inches from my eyes." The guest sets out, hoping that with his friend's directions he will find his way through the neighborhood by running his hand along the walls and fences, but of course he gets lost and ends up standing helplessly in the fogbank. "Just above me I could make out a jet of gas which I guessed came from a street lamp, and I moved over to that, and, while I tried to recover my bearings, kept my hand on the iron post. Except for this flicker of gas, no larger than the tip of my finger, I could distinguish nothing about me." Rarely has the intimate interplay of gaslight and fog been so precisely described.

God bless [the lamplighter]! For the term of his twilight diligence is
near at hand; and for not much longer shall we watch him speeding
up the street and, at measured intervals, knocking another luminous
hole into the dusk.

—ROBERT LOUIS STEVENSON, "A Plea for Gas Lamps"

Long after a new epoch had begun, the charms of Victorian life lived on in the realm of popular entertainment. Patrick Hamilton, whose novels such as *Hangover Square* are very much a part of the aggressive tristesse of the 1930s, also wrote a then-famous play, *Gaslight* (1938), subtitled "A Victorian Thriller in Three Acts." A minor technical detail gives the play its glow: in a house with gas lighting, turning up the gas in one room would cause a gas flame already burning in another room to dwindle slightly. The great scene at the end of *Gaslight*'s first act reveals that "gaslight" is not merely an auratic metaphor for the gloomy house and Mrs. Manningham's gloomy life; it is part of the plot's ingenious machinery: "What's the matter, Mrs. Manningham?"—"Quiet! Be quiet! He has come back! Look! Look at the light! It is going down! Wait!" (*Pause, as light sinks.*) "Dear me, now. How very odd that is. How very odd indeed." And in the third act, as salvation draws near, the paternal detective Rough, coming to Mrs. Manningham's aid, plays his own little game of cat and mouse with the evil husband: "Excuse me,

Manningham, but do you get the same impression as myself?"—"What impression?"—"An impression that the light is going down in this room."—"I have not noticed it." —"Yes... surely... There.... (*The light goes slowly down*) —eerie, isn't it? Now we are almost in the dark.... Why do you think that has happened? You don't suppose a light has been put on somewhere else? You don't suppose that strangers have entered the house?"

You don't suppose that strangers have entered the house? Here the question echoes tentatively from the early twentieth century back into the nineteenth, and it reverberates with our neo-Victorian pleasure in horror. We still enjoy subjecting ourselves for a while to the feeling that "strangers have entered the house," but we also long for the long-lost assurance that nothing will befall us, that in the end the light will burn calmly once again. The present has long since ceased to offer any guarantee of that. The gaslight glows across to us with the strangely nebulous nimbus of an uncanny age that—long ago—promised security all the same.

—Oh ! Maintenant, reprit le premier interlocuteur, il nous reste…

—Quoi ? demanda un autre.

—Le crime…

—Voilà un mot qui a toute la hauteur d'une potence et toute la
profondeur de la Seine.

—BALZAC, *La Peau de Chagrin*

This uncanniness concentrated itself at certain canonical
points of the epoch. We live in a world full of carnage and
atrocities, yet we must admit that we enjoy perusing certain
readily graspable "cases" from the history of crime, rather
like mystery novels. Perhaps it is because their sinister nature
is clearly bounded and relatively trivial compared to the
overwhelming horror of the mass murder wreaked by wars
and dictatorships—and perhaps because they buttress the
illusion that all horrors can still be combated with the tools
of investigative reason. The very word "case," in which law
and medicine intersect, has something soothing about it. It
establishes a clear contour: case by case the terror, the murderous transgression, is unambiguously outlined, it has a
beginning and an end, and an explanation—at least it is
supposed to have one. It is instructive to call to mind the
criminal cases that have gained the status of a *cause célèbre*,
of a legendary example. Each nation has its own chronicle;
but internationally, of all the murder cases of the past two

hundred years, probably none has held the same fascination in posterity's mythopoetic recollection as a certain unsolved series of murders in London in the year 1888. The interest in these murders, which claimed the lives of five or six prostitutes in the East End of the city between August and November, and whose perpetrator called himself "Jack the Ripper" in several jocular letters to the public, seems inexhaustible. The murders featured the systematic mutilation of the women's bodies, culminating with the victim Mary Kelly (the only one found not in an East End alley, with the unpredictable risk of passersby, but in a private room, where the murderer could take his time): her breasts were cut off, her heart and kidneys were removed, and her body parts were arranged symmetrically on a table.

The figure of "Jack," in many different forms, soon found its way into literature. As early as 1926 Alfred Hitchcock filmed Marie Belloc Lowndes's 1913 novel *The Lodger*—the first of a whole series of films inviting the audience to guess whether an eccentric lodger was a harmless bachelor or Jack the Ripper. With all its bizarrely grisly details, suffused by the auratic gaslight of a Belle-Époque metropolis and its foggy slums, the affair was tailor-made for the salacious speculations of the dilettante, and there is a long list of hypothetical perpetrators nominated by assiduous amateurs: a freemason or a gorilla, a midwife or a Jewish butcher, a vivisectionist or an occultist (Aleister Crowley casually spread the rumor that the murders were committed by Madame Blavatsky). The murderer was said to be the Duke of Clarence—or the Crown Prince himself (later Edward VII). In mystery novels and films, Sherlock Holmes was sent in pursuit of the Ripper; in 1978, Michael Dibdin made Holmes himself the murderer (*The Last Sherlock Holmes Story*) in what seems a dark pulp fiction variant on the Oedipus theme: the tale of the avenger who himself has committed the evil deed whose curse rests upon the city. The echoes are far-reaching: Mack the Knife is unthinkable without Jack the Ripper, as is William Kramps, "*l'homme qui éventre les bouchers*," in Marcel Carné's *Drôle de Drame*. The English serial killer Peter Sutcliffe, who committed his crimes between 1975 and 1981, was quickly dubbed "The Yorkshire Ripper," though his weapon of choice was the hammer. Again and again he managed to elude the longest and most elaborate police operation in British history—he was interviewed no fewer than nine times, without arousing suspicion, before a complete fluke finally led to his arrest. The police hampered their own investigation with a disastrous penchant for projecting the historic Jack the Ripper pattern onto the series of murders at hand. They were bent on searching for a prostitute-killer, although Sutcliffe murdered women in general, merely including the occasional prostitute. One of the most recent attempts to solve the riddle of the Ripper is quite telling: the perpetrator is claimed to be the painter Walter Sickert (1860–1942), a pupil of Whistler and a friend of Degas, whose stature is shown by the fact that seven of his paintings were displayed at the very start of the Royal Academy's major exhibition "British Art in the Twentieth Century." His influence reaches from the post-Impressionist realism of the "Camden Town Group" all the way to Bloomsbury.

Patricia Cornwell, author of the book that attempts to convict Sickert, has written a spectacularly successful series of mysteries (the first, *Postmortem*, appearing in 1990) whose heroine is the pathologist Kay Scarpetta. It is strange how the activities of fictional characters lend authority to their inventors. (Conan Doyle was occasionally asked to intervene in the investigation of mysterious crimes, as though Sherlock Holmes could whisper the solution in his ear.) Now Patricia Cornwell proceeds to solve the great riddle, claiming that her book reveals the unambiguous historical truth. Its title is *Portrait of a Killer: Jack the Ripper—Case Closed* (2002)—a claim made on the basis of a few scant results from forensic investigations which she herself instigated. It is extremely hard to believe that the historic material, inevitably highly contaminated, permits a comparison between DNA from the stamps and envelope flaps of several of the Ripper's letters on the one hand, and various of Sickert's letters and smocks on the other; there is not a word on these methodological issues. Supposedly the comparison is not intended to enable a direct identification, but to document a certain shared DNA profile which occurs only in one percent of the population. Surprisingly, this knock-down argument is covered in half a page, in passing and rather bashfully. No details are given, no scientific evidence is presented, no verifiable results are shared—and the entire book contains not a single piece of genuine documentary evidence (assuming one does not choose to apply the term to the comparison—a stylistic absurdity—between a doodle by the Ripper and a stick figure drawn by Sickert). Despite all the courtroom anecdotes she relates, the author has no notion of scientific analysis. The truly staggering thing about the book is the brazen naivety with which she seeks to take a painter's interest in music halls and the eroticism of the demimonde and make it into a rope to hang him.

A good murder is a great godsend.

—THACKERAY, "Solitude in September," 1833

Walter Sickert was known for living the classic life of an artistic bohemian, and (after pursuing an acting career of his own for several years) as someone with a passionate predilection for vaudeville—for cheap, shadily erotic music halls, the English equivalent to the Moulin Rouge milieu. He shared this predilection with countless other artists, writers, and dilettantes, with Wilde and Beerbohm, Arthur Symons and Ernest Dowson. Cornwell takes it as a substantial piece of evidence for his guilt in a series of sex murders. And what's more, the man painted lots of naked women, and some of these pictures are clearly suggestive. "I noticed murky images of clothed men reflected in mirrors inside gloomy bedrooms where nude women sit on iron bedsteads. I saw impending violence and death.... I saw a diabolically creative mind, and I saw evil." And the reader hears foolishness talking itself into a frenzy. One of the pictures she mentions is well-known to art historians: *The Camden Town Affair* (1909). It shows an austere room with a bed where a naked woman lies motionless. A man stands by the bed with folded arms, gazing down at her. It is the title, rather than anything explicitly depicted, that connects the painting with the murder of a prostitute two years previously; it caused a scandal when it was exhibited. Sickert painted several variations on this painting, and its ambiguity is shown by the fact that parallel versions were entitled *What Shall We Do for the Rent?* and *Summer Afternoon*. The painting from 1909, which Sickert described as an exercise in the contrast between clothed and naked flesh, was purchased by Paul Signac.

Virginia Woolf once wrote about Sickert's paintings: "It is difficult to look at them and not to invent a plot." Indeed, Patricia Cornwell demonstrates the truth of these words—but did she really look at the paintings? Is she even capable of looking at a painting? She has no interest in Sickert's rich and complex oeuvre (an oeuvre with a dark palette of earth tones, the work of a painter who seems enamored of the touching luster of all that is shabby, cheap, and neglected, an oeuvre that includes many depictions that can be seen as showing solidarity or even tenderness toward these destitute women—women who appear as subjects, not merely as the objects of male desire). She is interested only in extremely specific features of his work that seem to fit into her model. For instance, the sketches of individual parts or sections of the body, found in the work of nearly every painter interested in depicting the human figure, become signs of an urge to mutilate. Looking at art history, that would make a very long list of sex murderers. Whatever is expressed by these depictions of "gloomy bedrooms"—a sexual power fantasy, or the ironic presentation thereof; a lustful dream or discomfort, even alarm at this lust—it cannot be articulated as precisely as the author thinks. She is probably unable to comprehend that an image can possess a certain ambiguity, indeed that this very ambiguity can constitute its charm and its stature. The naturalistic novelist George Moore wrote: "Nature has gifted Mr. Sickert with a keen hatred of the commonplace." But however persistently the artist may seek to achieve complexity—his unmasker reduces it all to one-dimensionality. These pictures of gloomy, shabby rooms may merely seek to capture a mood, as articulated by the title of what is probably Sickert's most famous painting, at the Tate Gallery: *Ennui*.

Forensic pathology is currently experiencing a peculiar apotheosis. It can turn into a grotesque form of political theater, as witnessed several years ago in Germany when the bizarre fate of the brain of Red Army Faction terrorist Ulrike Meinhof was revealed; doctors had brazenly preserved it in secret, dissecting it in an attempt to bolster a theory of revolution as a disease. In our event culture pathology can become a perverse form of entertainment: Professor Gunther von Hagens, never without his hat, performing a public autopsy for paying guests. In crime novels, pathology suddenly appears as something like the last, most naive hope, now that the genre itself has lost faith in all the authorities classically trusted to ascertain the truth. For a long, long time now, crime novels have portrayed the police as corrupt, the secret services as monstrous, the detective as an impotent neurotic or a powerless low-level bureaucrat. But the scalpel never lies, and suddenly it is once again capable of anything. Now that all the crime genre's constructions of heroism and justice have crumbled, we are seeing a revival of the sort of pure science that vanished from the genre long ago, with R. Austin Freeman's Dr. Thorndyke, say, who debuted in 1907. (The imperturbably subaltern supporting role of the forensic specialist Moers in his lab on the Quai des Orfèvres in the Maigret novels was typical of the classic detective stories.) Now, for one strange moment, science has once again become the great white hope of the crime novel.

The dull, clumsy, repetitive Kay Scarpetta novels by Patricia Cornwell, who—it is now customary in the genre—attempts to cover up her mediocrity with exaggerated, kinky violence (while selling the image of a strong woman bent on revenge), represent a trendy genre variation of only moderate interest. The author's pompous claim to have discovered a historic enigma's definitive solution using simulated expert knowledge would hardly be worthy of notice. But the extent of the autodidact's recklessness and her boundless self-assurance—"Case Closed"—inspire a kind of horror at a vitriolic portrayal that twists each detail to make it seem suspicious, showing that there are still people actually capable of taking a painter's dissolute life, and the fact that he produced disturbing paintings of whores' cheerless rooms, as serious grounds for suspicion.

GESCHWITZ: *How dark it is here!*
SCHIGOLCH: *It shall get much darker yet.*

—ALBAN BERG, *Lulu*, adapted from the plays *Earth Spirit* and *Pandora's Box* by Frank Wedekind

After watching Berg's opera, the opera stage feels like Jack the Ripper's natural habitat. How many operas culminate in a woman's death! How many of these deaths are murders! Let us leave aside the splendid suicides—poison, a leap onto the pyre or from the Castel Sant'Angelo—let us discount the executions, often enough ("Have this woman killed!") barely distinguishable from murder: for one moment, let us reflect solely on what is done to a woman by a man, just one man, in private. On this strange form of love that seems essential to opera, a form that gives special truth to the adage that every work of art must have a woman's corpse walled up in its foundation. It is not for nothing that operas often end with the flashing of a knife—"Eh bien, damnée!... Vous pouvez m'arrêter, c'est moi qui l'ai tuée. Ah! ma Carmen! ma Carmen adorée!"

This murderous knife flashes in both of Alban Berg's operas. "Marie: How red is the rising moon! Wozzeck: Like bloody iron! (*draws a knife*)" This is echoed by Jack's words in *Lulu*: "We don't need a lamp, there's moonlight." In the light of this baleful moon Wozzeck stabs his wife to death, and from then on sees nothing but blood—a man driven to madness by life and by jealousy. Lulu, as the protagonist, turns this story on its head, taking us behind the looking glass. We see her as the self-assured arouser of jealousy; only at the very end does a man with a knife come in to stop her. This man is not mad; his monstrosity lies in the fact that he seems to be the only one whose sanity has gone untouched. Lulu's power makes no impression on him, and for a moment ("Good evening! Good evening!") he nearly walks out on her.

the blood that's thick, the spot that's wet
the suitcase and the carving set
the ink is deep the morning heady
on the table breakfast's ready

—ROR WOLF, "neue nachrichten"

After Lulu's death cry has died away, after the door opens
and Jack reemerges to plunge "a blood-stained knife into
the Countess Geschwitz's body," he says another four lines.
"That was quite a piece of work!" as he cheerfully washes
his hands. "I'm such a lucky devil, damn it!" Here he looks
around for a towel. "These people don't even have towels!"
and then: "And you're not long for this world either." This
he says in passing to the dying Countess Geschwitz. The
officious washing of the hands—Pilate, a workman after the
day's work, a doctor after the operation—suggests how
much blood has flowed, evokes the physical, brutish, fetishistic procedure. If we recall the specter of the historical
Jack—and how soon after his murders this play was written
(beginning in 1892), how intimately Wedekind felt connected to this story!—we know what he was doing behind
that door. There, to live up to his name, he had to mutilate
and eviscerate the woman's body.

 After such a task, to shake his head over "these people"
who don't even have towels is a lurid flash of Wedekind's

humor. But the greatest, most chilling line is the contemplative, triumphant "I'm such a lucky devil, damn it!" Here the very thing that Lulu ceaselessly, unthinkingly lives out, love as the destruction of the other, becomes a triumphalist program, in words whose cheerful vulgarity makes us shudder because it evokes what we all long for: luck. This line, uttered between the washing of the hands and the search for the towel, has to be a gleeful one: a genuine sense of happiness now that the thirst for blood is quenched.

Woman is constantly, Man only intermittently sexual.
—OTTO WEININGER

When the male's intermittent sexuality does manifest itself, it is most convenient for him to avail himself of a prostitute. But she does not love her clients; it cannot be demanded of her, yet the man never forgives her for it. The murder of prostitutes sets the seal to this resentment, and this is the form taken by Lulu's ultimate elimination. In the end the woman's oceanic power must be cut down to size. Tellingly, the execution cannot take place until life has once again forced Lulu to prostitute herself openly. She originally comes from the street, as we are told in the first act, but when we see her onstage, she is no longer forced to practice "vice" professionally. Until the very end. Now she must haggle over a single coin, when previously enormous sums were dealt with in passing. That the more ardently she addresses the client ("You've nothing to worry about from me. I like you so much!") the more he seems to hesitate is part of the logic of the profession. That is the last thing she says before her death cry, repeated four times: No!

Prostitution, and the bourgeoisie's vitriolic abhorrence of it, forms the central theme of Karl Kraus's reflections on eroticism and morality (*Sittlichkeit und Kriminalität*). We find a significant, if sometimes awkward echo of his thoughts in a newspaper article written by Kurt Weill in 1926: "Wedekind's characters are flogged on by their passions, revealed in all their brutal egotism. But these passion-wrenched people are integrated into nature's eternal laws, and their libidinousness, taken to the point of shameless depravity, is, in its original, undistorted form, desirable and moral. This dichotomy—this longing and its false fulfillment—made Wedekind into a polemicist. He fights for the right to freely control one's own body, he rages against the commercialized untouchability of women, against the abhorrence of the whore."

This epitomizes the sexual morality of Karl Kraus's

polemics and Wedekind's drama: they condemn the bourgeois society that dares to despise the whore. The uniqueness of Wedekind's strategy is that, in so doing, he sets up the whore as the destroyer of the world.

Even greater was the excitement an hour later when a man whose face was made up to resemble a skull stood on the corner of Wentworth and Commercial streets and shouted "I am Jack the Ripper!"

—TOM CULLEN, *Autumn of Terror*

In the film by G. W. Pabst (*Pandora's Box*, 1928), we see a Jack who enters looking hounded, with beads of sweat on his face. In this way (as with Jack and Lulu's strange kiss: "The mistletoe above you—symbol of salvation and forgiveness"), Pabst, probably concerned to avoid alienating his audience, sought to sentimentalize the character. The confrontation between Jack and Lulu becomes the encounter of two lost souls, two extremes that tenderly touch for one moment. To wonderful cinematic effect, this romanticizes Wedekind's Jack, whom Pabst shows as a handsome man, softening the edges of the crass, crude figure full of mysterious brutality. Reading Wedekind's (and Berg's) stage directions for Jack's first appearance, a single detail exposes the compromise made by Pabst's film—the "fiery red hands with gnawed fingernails." These gnawed nails do not seem to be a sign of insecurity, any more than the "inflamed eyes" constitute a weakness: both are the ciphers for a consuming heat that rises from this figure, and for the insatiable activity of the greedy gaze and a hunger that, in a pinch, makes him gnaw on himself.

With Jack's appearance, the play comes full circle: he is the reincarnation of the animal tamer who appears in the prologue. With great rigor, Wedekind, who liked to write for the circus ring (for instance a large-scale pantomime for Zirkus Renz), transformed the moral institution of the theater back into a show booth in which morals had no role to play. In Wedekind's prologue, Lulu is carried in by a stagehand at the command of the animal tamer—"Hey, August, go and fetch our snake!"—and warned ("My sweet beast"): "You have no right to yowl and hiss / and sully the image of female bliss, / Or with faces and shenanigans / To spoil the childish innocence of sins!" The play is dominated by this circus atmosphere: cold, grotesque, with almost Brechtian distancing effects and sideshow marionettes. Theodor Adorno wrote of Berg's opera: "The horrifying scene with Schön's death is a sketch with grotesque clowns, who crouch behind all sorts of props and, when discovery threatens, begin to turn somersaults."

Yet in its musical continuum, constructed with rigorous symmetry, one hears an inescapably *unifying* force that contrasts with the grotesquely fragmented composition of Wedekind's play. Hanns Eisler pointed out regretfully that the composer had made Wedekind's "lurid penny-dreadful filled with brilliant details into a work of late Romantic opera that fails to avoid Wagnerian clichés in its presentation of the characters." He complained that all the comedy had been obliterated. "Despite Alban Berg's mastery, despite his truly noble efforts, any halfway rational listener would have to ... burst out laughing when, for instance, the newspaper magnate, in the midst of a tempestuous fit of jealousy, yells 'I have to go to the Stock Exchange!' That sort of thing is quite funny, after all. But Alban Berg's music does not permit detachment or laughter; instead, it demands that the viewer constantly empathize with the conflicts of his opera characters, which are to be understood abstractly, as universally human conflicts ('Human, we are all human ...')." ("On the Relation between Text and Music: Notes for a Seminar on Hegel").

Dr. Schön's words, paraphrased by Eisler, are actually: "You know I must go to the Stock Exchange today." These sorts of statements crop up quite often. "At the editorial office everyone's at a loss for what to write ..." They provide the backdrop of the bourgeois existence against which Lulu's primal feminine essence stands out; stock exchange and editors fade before the fury of urge-driven fate. The grotesqueness of this contrast is only half-maintained in the dialogues adapted from Wedekind; on the musical level, what unfolds is a deeper solemnity. "You implacable doom!"

Ho dritto anch'io d'agir com' altr' uomo…

—*I Pagliacci*

Jack is the end point. In the seminal Vienna staging of 1905, initiated by Karl Kraus, he was played by Wedekind himself. Jack is the one who cuts Lulu down to size. He is bourgeois society's ultima ratio against the oceanically surging, all-dissolving libidinous being.

We know nothing about Jack. But the stage directions describe him with far more detail than all the characters. None of the suffering, raging people who previously crossed Lulu's path were dignified with a precise description on their first appearance. Now someone enters the stage invested with a stupendous extravagance of painterly detail. This does not make him into an individual, however: the thick description only underlines the character's enigmatic nature, in which, though everything is seen with preternatural clarity, the details do not add up to a figure. "He is a stocky man, elastic in his movements, with a pale face, inflamed eyes, thick, arched eyebrows, drooping moustache, Van Dyke beard, shaggy side-whiskers, and fiery red hands with gnawed fingernails. He stares at the ground. He wears a dark overcoat and a small round felt hat." This has the peculiar intensity of a wanted poster, yet the fugitive seems impossible to grasp. It is as though the author sought to pin down a historical phenomenon which even by the inception of the play's first version (1892, only four years after the murders) had accrued all kinds of legends, lending it a form at once utterly concrete and doubly elusive in this concreteness. Jack's face was evidently one of the first seeds around which the Lulu tragedy crystallized, perhaps the very first dream image that appeared to the author; as early as January 1894 Wedekind noted: "a confiscated face, an outright belly-slitter." *Bauchaufschneider*, that was the name for the Ripper in German; clearly the author decided quite early on that Lulu's end would be her encounter with this man, and with his name.

What is the point of the description? To demonstrate that this man is ugly, or rather: that he has no need of beauty, no more than of wealth or any quality other than his somnambulistically sure monomania. His clothing, especially his hat, suggests a petty-bourgeois white-collar worker (which his first lines also oddly seem to fit: "I haven't any time, I must get home.... But you will have to give me back half the money, so that tomorrow I have enough for the omnibus"); he could be a subaltern civil servant—a police assistant, or the executioner. But once he comes into his own, he stands as a man of action, speaking of a "piece of work" which he savors in retrospect.

Looking at the evidence, one could imagine that from 1888 onward Wedekind's actual yearning was to write a Jack the Ripper play, that he conceived the long double tragedy *Earth Spirit/Pandora's Box* solely to serve as exposition for the moment when "Lulu opens the door and lets Jack into the room."

Don't let me beg any longer.

—Lulu to Jack

Like Wedekind, Berg lets Countess Geschwitz have the last word; if we can believe the playwright, she is the true "tragic heroine" of the second play. But in Berg's version her last words are "In eternity," while in Wedekind they are "Oh, damn it!" Berg leaves out these two words, which in the theatrical version follow "I am near to you! Will stay near—in eternity!": "(*Elbows collapsing*): Oh, damn it!—(*She dies*)."

Why did Berg, otherwise adhering so faithfully to the text of the play, omit these words, which are given such prominence? Does the erasure of the play's last words mean that in the opera pure passion prevails unyielding, as the figure whose hair Jack tousled distractedly, "like a dog," is allowed to utter one last, final evocation of romantic love? She, the "poor beast," as Jack casually remarks while petting her? It is she, in her boundless, hopeless love, who is not a beast—the beast, of course, is Lulu, whose murder seems ironically prefigured in the words of the prologue: "The soulless creature… / Tamed by human genius." Whether women have a soul is an ancient theological question. The only person who would claim that Lulu has a soul is Countess Geschwitz. That is precisely what makes her a tragic figure.

Pure tragedy is not permitted here, and it is this character, just before her exitus, who provides one of the strangest comic moments. In the interval between Jack's locking the door and Lulu's death cry, Geschwitz says, "as though in a dream" that she wants to go back to Germany now. "I'll enroll in the university. I must fight for women's rights, study law." (These are precisely the aspirations that earn women

Karl Kraus's most passionate scorn, judging from his writings in *Die Fackel*—ambitions that cause a self-assured being with a higher, deeper nature to stoop to pursuing a career, denaturing herself as a suffragette and academic.) It is so obvious that behind these locked doors an execution is taking place against which there is no legal appeal—and that makes these academic plans an unparalleled example of tragicomedy.

The play begins in sophisticated circles and then descends into shadiness. To master Lulu, society must ultimately call in a figure that does not belong to the beau-monde, or even the demimonde. Nor the "underworld," at most in an Acherontic sense. Jack comes from the un-world. And yet he is historic; he is the only historic figure in Lulu's story. The destroyer of prostitutes. The embodiment of a real historic phenomenon: the delight in the destruction of the woman as an openly sexual being.

The Bomb
What a Beautiful Breach in the World!

I have since tried to decide what the sound was like and couldn't. It wasn't like thunder or any kind of gun or any other sound I had ever heard. It wasn't a thud or a bang or a boom; it was just a loud noise. . . . He had no face left. I had never seen anything like it.

—REX STOUT, *A Family Affair* (1975)

IN 1896, on one of his tireless journeys to promote his project for a Jewish state, Theodor Herzl came to Paris and called on the great Edmond Rothschild to urge his support. He met with uncomprehending resistance, however, and the two men parted on chilly terms. Herzl noted the following detail of their farewell in his diary: "Rothschild"—who had asked two friends to be present at their conference—"detained the other two by their coat buttons; I think, he had asked them there for his protection, in case I turned out to be an anarchist." (July 19, 1896) This may be slightly facetious, an exaggerated explanation for a rich man's nervousness when faced with a petitioner who could, in his own fashion, be quite impertinent. The extremely broad use of the word "anarchist" recalls Orwell's remark that in the 1920s the diffusely anxious English bourgeoisie tended to refer to Cubist paintings or vegetarian meals as being "Bolshevism." All the same, the specter of anarchism, the nervous penchant for seeing "anarchists" and hearing explosions everywhere, is a signature of the epoch—the threat was perceived as ubiquitous.

For a time, the terms anarchism and nihilism were used almost interchangeably. Anarchy is non-dominion, the freedom from dominion, its abolition, the society without dominion. *Nihil* is nothingness. The concept of nihilism has quite an interesting and unexpected history, beginning long before Turgenev's novel *Fathers and Sons*, in 1862, presented the first literary treatment of the concept as the watchword of a generation that "bows before no authority" and sees negation as the "most useful" thing. In this strict sense, nihilism is the utilitarian rejection of all that tradition holds as binding. This is summed up with exquisite humor in Leonid Leonov's wonderful *Notes of a Small-Town Man* (1922): "In our town, Gogulyov, there lived a petty bourgeois by the name of Zozulnikov. He was quite an insignificant fellow (in a certain sense even an adulterer in his relationship to his landlady). Suddenly he set himself up as an anarchist,

hanging a little sign in the window saying 'I recognize nothing whatsoever period Alexander Zozulnikov.' I go to Father
Gennadii—I say, so on and so forth, an anarchist has turned
up. He explained to me that those are people who think
there ought to be nothing, roughly speaking." Yet long
before that, surprisingly enough even in Hegel's writings,
nihilism did in fact revolve around absolute nothingness.
The question "Why is there something and not nothing?"
is one of the famous touchstones that reveal whether someone has a philosophical bent. But if we look more closely,
nothingness also proves to be a favorite subject for popular
entertainment.

Gershon Legman's astonishing work *The Rationale of the
Dirty Joke* is an analytical encyclopedia of naughty jokes
compiled by a brilliant dilettante who scrupulously noted
his sources ("Transcontinental train, told by a St. Louis
attorney, 1943") and drew numerous comparisons with early
modern and Middle Eastern comic fables and folktale narratives. The first volume (1968) devotes an entire section to
stories in which a visitor to a brothel is offered a mysterious
erotic specialty with a suggestive but utterly cryptic name
(*le diligence de Lyon* or *the sleeve job*). After excruciatingly
long delays and complications the story ends without
a punch line, in nothingness—the customer has a fatal
accident, the woman never shows up; one way or the other,

we never learn how to decipher the mysterious offer. There are several such stories that heighten the tension to the extreme, only to leave the protagonist (and the reader) dangling in the void; in all probability, they originally circulated orally before taking on their classic form, as it were, in some magazine story. The story of a man traveling in a foreign city who casually presents a message he has been given but cannot read himself—and everyone who sees it turns pale or red with anger; he is cursed at, he is thrown out, people break off relations with him, he is expelled from the country and has no idea why. The same thing happens to him at home when he tries to have the ill-fated message translated— no one will tell him a thing, everyone turns away from him... (Cleveland Moffett, "The Mysterious Card"). A woman travels with her mother to Paris, where they find a quiet, old-fashioned hotel that has only two single rooms left. She lies down for a bit, getting up half an hour later to check in on her mother—but the room is empty, unoccupied. At the front desk she is told: But *Mademoiselle*, you were traveling alone... (Ralph Straus, "The Most Maddening Story in the World"). Legman tackles the subject with clinical earnestness, maintaining that all these enigmatic tales with their central, unfillable void can be traced back, in a very elementary "aesthetic" sense, to castration anxiety. Psychoanalysis famously posited the alarming quality of the "hole" as an essential factor of male psychology: the fear caused by the sight of the female genitals, where something crucial seems to be missing. In a famous scene, Shakespeare shows Hamlet's conversation revolving with courtly obscenity around this "nothing." The characters are taking their seats to watch the play within the play. "Lady, shall I lie in your lap?" Hamlet asks his Ophelia. "No, my lord." "I mean, my head upon your lap?" "Ay, my lord." "Do you think I meant country matters?" "I think nothing, my lord." "That's a fair thought to lie between maid's legs." "What is, my lord?" "Nothing." *Nothing* is what lies between the legs of a virgin, bringing us to *country matters* after all—to the ingenuous vulgarity of peasant life.

Nothingness and disappearance, even more so than apparitions, are the primal substance of ghost stories, which tap in to very old fears. And as a form the detective story always aims in the end at the effect of an unsettling invisibility: the seemingly unbridgeable gap in the chain of logic. These are the pièces de résistance of the mystery genre—the murder weapon that cannot be found ("The Tea Leaf"), the corpse that vanishes despite the strictest surveillance, the mysterious house that is not there the next morning ("The Lamp of God"), and of course the invisible murderer: the inexplicable murder in a hermetically sealed room. The *locked room murder*, the construction of an unsolvable puzzle that is

186

solved in the end after all, has spurred writers' and readers' ambitions over and over again. In a classic example of the form by one of its great specialists, John Dickson Carr (*The Hollow Man*, 1935), Dr. Fell gives a famous speech on this problem's variations. Of course the supernatural cannot be permitted to intrude, even if it may appear to be the riddle's only solution, suffusing the story with eerie suggestiveness. By technological or psychological means (the victim was murdered just before the inaccessible room was locked, or just after it was opened up) the silhouette of the invisible is suddenly rendered perceptible. In his great novel *The Invisible Man*, H. G. Wells approached this sort of esthesis from a different angle, that of invisibility: the man who has made himself invisible, one of the great mad scientists of horror literature, not only has all kinds of difficulties in moving undetected around other people (difficulties with great comic potential, as he must venture out naked or wrapped grotesquely in bandages), initially he has trouble going up or down stairs, as he is unable to see his own feet...

Detective stories construct a seemingly unsolvable riddle, followed by a triumphant payoff demonstrating the most elegant possible solution to the unsolvable. Legman pointed out in passing that in a sense the time-travel paradoxes of science fiction provide the same aesthetic satisfaction as the locked room murders. The narrative genres of the mystery, the ghost story, the science fiction time paradox, the shaggy-dog story and the dirty joke about an inconceivable brothel specialty revolve around ideal forms of vanishing or void. These variations are childishly "nihilistic" in the sense that they adeptly and casually inscribe the structure of reality with a "nothing," a zero, a hole. Is it meaningful to draw a remote analogy between this end point of genre fantasies and the *nihil* manifested in the explosion of a bomb? The *tertium comparationis* would be the sudden disappearance, or, more abstractly, the radical suspension of what is thought to be possible. The task of the typical riddling detective novel is to present one such crack, one such hole, one such breach, to construct the impossible crime that unhinges the world's logic, so that the detective can demonstrate the curative force of the deductions which restore logical harmony to the world. But the explosion of the nihilist bomb, with its new logic, is irreversible. The comparison clearly demonstrates that the riddle posed by the bomb cannot be solved, that it resists solution.

something rots in the sky, it swells and corrodes,
sweats and festers and brews in this tableau.

the baron locked his cabinet sound
as the city sank swiftly into the ground.
—ROR WOLF, "waldmanns hut"

On March 19, 1881, in response to the assassination of Tsar
Alexander II, the leading German anarchist Johann Most
wrote an editorial entitled "Long Live Tyrannicide!" in his
newspaper *Freiheit*: "Victory! Victory! The word of the
poet is fulfilled." (This refers to the article's epigraph, by the
poet C. Beck: "Arrest this man, arrest that man; / One of
them will reach you all the same." "C. Beck" is probably Karl
Isidor Beck, 1817–1879, author of the *Lieder vom armen
Manne* [Songs about the Poor Man, 1846].) "One of Europe's
most vicious tyrants"—Most continued—"whose doom had
long since been sealed and who, in wild fits of vengeance,
had countless heroes and heroines of the Russian people
exterminated or imprisoned—the Russian Emperor is no
more.... Five times the scoundrel had managed to brush
the boundary of the Beyond with his coat sleeve; once again
he was prating of the 'finger of God' that had supposedly
just saved his cursed life, when the fist of the people shut
his mouth once and for all." The fist of the people counters

the finger of God. Most, his clumsy rhetoric driven by implacable hatred, describes the assassination. The first "dynamite bomb" destroys only Alexander's carriage and several courtiers; the would-be assassin is already seized, "and those surrounding the Emperor, sporting uniform braids and pigtails, utterly consumed by corruption, heave a sigh of relief at what they believe is a threat averted. Just then another bomb comes flying; this time it falls at the despot's feet, shatters his legs, tears open his abdomen. . . . The bystanders seem paralyzed, it is only the resolute bomb thrower who keeps his head and manages to flee. The Emperor is carried to his palace, where for another hour and a half, in agonizing pain, he is able to reflect on his crime-filled life. At last he bites the dust.—These, for now, are the simple facts of the matter." The "resolute bomb thrower" is a phrasing whose sensationalizing tone expresses admiration for the "deed," and the very vein in which the "simple facts of the matter" are depicted contains a world of hate-filled rage. "For us this terror is an exquisite pleasure . . . Who is wretch enough to actually mourn the death of such a monster?"

The revolt against despotism, especially in Russia, arose from a noble wrath at injustice, but this rebellion at once took on peculiar traits, in particular a kind of fashionable vanity. Dostoevsky's *Demons* (1872) is the diabolical caricature of a narrowly bounded social movement, written *cum ira et studio* and certainly not with the intent of passing down a balanced depiction, but the novel presciently captures two things: the absolutely abstract nature of the nihilists' "political" intervention, as they lacked almost all contact with the masses to whom they felt allied, and the utopian delight in the obliteration (not the alteration) of the objectionable status quo, the delight in annihilation.

One of the finest features of this great and unjust novel is the way the author's satiric depiction of the foolish liberal Stepan Trofimovich, embodying the pre-nihilism generation and its progressive fantasies, takes on a quality of sheer tenderness. One vignette from the beginning of the novel must suffice here: the aging scholar lives in the fear that the government could put him under surveillance and persecute him for a poem he wrote many years ago in Berlin; at the same time, the authorship of this manuscript, with several copies in circulation, fills him with great pride. Finally the narrator summarizes the poem for the reader, and this masterful caricature of a "subversive" work, simultaneously illustrating the vanity of the intellectual, the literary fashions of the 1830s, and the paranoia of the state that could feel threatened by such effusions, is an apogee of comedy in nineteenth-century literature.

I find it difficult to give the plot, because to tell the truth
I understand nothing of it. It is some sort of allegory, in
lyrical-dramatic form, resembling the second part of
Faust.... All these choruses sing about something very
indefinite, mostly about somebody's curse, but with a
tinge of higher humor. Then suddenly the scene changes,
and some sort of "Festival of Life" begins, in which even
insects sing ... and, if I remember, a mineral—that is, an
altogether inanimate object—also gets to sing about
something. Generally, everyone sings incessantly, and if
they speak, they squabble somehow indefinitely, but
again with a tinge of higher meaning....Suddenly a youth
of indescribable beauty rides in on a black horse, followed
by a terrible multitude of all the nations. The youth represents death, and all the nations yearn for it. Finally...
the Tower of Babel suddenly appears and some athletes
finally finish building it with a song of new hope, and
when they have built to the very top, the proprietor of,
shall we say, Olympus flees in comical fashion, and quick-
witted mankind takes over his place and at once begins
a new life with a new perception of things.

Over the course of the novel this poem, this little scare-
crow hung with romantic, idealistic rags, takes on, in retrospect, a very peculiar physiognomy: Stefan Trofimovich's

silly utopian notion that power might "flee in comical
fashion" when the athletes of humanity strike up their song
of new hope may be laughable, but seems increasingly noble
by contrast to the murderous violence of nihilism. It is the
product of a foolishly good heart.

At one point in the vast collection of sketches and notes
for *The Demons*, Dostoevsky notes: "Nechaev is not a socialist but a rebel. His ideal is insurrection and destruction and
then, whatever might come." The crux of this attitude is
illuminated *ex negativo* at another point in the notes, in the
sketch for a conversation between the prince and the bishop:
"The Bishop proves to him that one must not make a leap,
but that one must rather regenerate the image of man in
oneself (through long-lasting work, and only then vault
ahead). 'So one can't do it all at once?' 'No, one can't. It
would only turn the work of angels into a work of the devil.'
The Prince: 'Alas, I knew that myself.' "

Planning his work in his notes, the author develops an
explicitly ideological critique that in the novel is almost
always conveyed with artful indirectness, in keeping with
his remark: "Special tone of the narrative. Most important,
the special tone of the narrative will save everything. The
tone consists in not explaining Nechaev or the Prince." The
hinge of the sketched-out conversation is the "all at once":
the yearning for an absolute rupture. The diffuse unrest that

can no longer be satisfied by any old change, only by *the*
change: the explosion.

*I thought I could free Russia. I heard men talk of Liberty one night in
a café. I had never heard the word before.*

—OSCAR WILDE, *Vera; or, The Nihilists*

Around the turn of the twentieth century English literature
produced several noteworthy narratives about terrorism.
They include two of the era's greatest novels, Joseph Conrad's *The Secret Agent* (1907) and *Under Western Eyes* (1911).
In a foreword to the latter book Conrad remarks: "The most
terrifying reflection (I am speaking now for myself) is that
all these people"—the terrorists—"are not the product of
the exceptional but of the general—of the normality of their
place, and time, and race." Compared to Conrad's passion-
ately cool moral gravity, there is something innocent about
Robert Louis Stevenson's artful, playful little fictions. Yet
again and again they too go to the explosive limit. The hole,
the "devouring circle," the zero: "Zero" is the name of the
title character in Stevenson's capriccio *The Dynamiter*—a
man condemned to produce infernal machines that never
work, despairing at his bombs' capricious refusal to explode

on time. Until in the end one functions after all, and tears
him to pieces. Again and again, in a highly peculiar mixture
of grotesqueness and gravity, Stevenson lets this bumbling
madman utter completely true statements: "Horrible was
the society with which we warred, but our own means were
not less horrible." And at one point he falls into lecturing
mode: "In this dark period of time, a star—the star of dynamite—has risen for the oppressed."

Certainly, as shown by military history, and the history
of Europe's urban catastrophes, there had been horrific
developments in explosives even earlier on. Next to the
plague and devastating conflagrations, the explosion of a
powder magazine was a classic disaster for an old European
city: in 1654 the explosion of the magazine "t'Secreet van
Hollandt" destroyed the center of Delft, killing many people, including the important painter Carel Fabritius; in 1819
the powder chamber exploded in the Château de Vincennes,
which was being used as a fortress (Alfred de Vigny, who
witnessed the incident, described it in the second book of
Servitude et grandeur militaires: "Suddenly both of my windows burst open instantaneously, and all their shattered
panes fell into my room with a pleasant silvery tinkle.")
Schiller incorporates the igniting of the power magazine as
a Gothic topos in *The Robbers* ("And presently the powder-
magazine blew up into the air with a crash as if the earth

were rent in twain, heaven burst to shivers, and hell sunk
ten thousand fathoms deeper"). The reverberating breach
in the world was an old threat, but dynamite, transportable,
practical and easy to manipulate, lent the danger of explosion a new dimension: that of expediency.

Dynamite, as we know, was invented in 1866 by Alfred
Nobel; faced with the destructive repercussions of his patent,
he later felt the need to exculpate himself by establishing prizes
for peace and idealism. Essentially, dynamite is a material
with the explosive power of nitroglycerine, which had been
known for some time, but lacking its capricious unpredict-
ability—nitroglycerine can be set off by the slightest tremor.
(In 1864 Nobel's Swedish factory exploded; one of the victims was his youngest brother.) Dynamite drastically altered
the possibilities for staging an explosion, which could now
be prepared much more easily, dependably, and practically.

Following the assassination of the tsar in 1881, an attempt
was made to kill the German Kaiser and the Crown Prince
with dynamite at the 1883 dedication of the Niederwald-
denkmal. (Located near Rüdesheim, this gigantic Germania
commemorated the foundation of the Reich and the war of
1870–71, "the unanimous ... uprising of the German people";
the Kaiser was the central figure of the huge bronze relief.)
The 1884 trial of the two chief suspects, August Reinsdorf
and Emil Küchler (executed in 1885), was documented by

Hugo Friedländer in *Interessante Kriminal-Prozesse* (Interesting Criminal Trials, III, 1912); as always, Friedländer's account has a special vividness because he attended the trial as a courtroom reporter and took down its crucial moments in shorthand. The dynamite, transported in a stoneware pot, was supposed to be ignited *en passant* with a glowing cigar. The co-defendant Rupsch, who was spared from execution, insisted to the court with muddled rationales (claiming he had only wanted to get a glimpse of the Kaiser and the Crown Prince) that he had thwarted the assassination attempt by using an *extinguished* cigar ("So with your cold cigar you blackened the fuse, in consequence of which the explosion did not take place?"). There is something plausibly practical about lighting the fuse of a dynamite charge with a cigar: the cigar is an unobtrusive prop, and has a bourgeois effect which can come in handy. The prop also seems to commend itself through the nonchalant gesture often demonstrated in westerns; the act of smoking lends a mysteriously casual touch to the fatal hand motion. In Holland, incidentally, this gesture features in an elegant patriotic myth from the gunpowder age: in 1831 the national hero J. C. J. van Speyk used his cigar to detonate the powder charge of the gunship under his command to keep the Dutch flag from falling into the hands of the Belgians (the classic painting by Jacobus Schoemaker-Doijer, *Van Speyk steekt zijn sigaar in het kruit*, from 1831–1832, is held by the Amsterdam Museum). Depending on the situation, the cigar can be aristocratic and dandyish or vulgar and rebellious, and it is the ideal instrument for setting off an explosion.

During the trial, the main defendant, Reinsdorf, spoke of the audacity of the oppressors and the misery of the working class, asking: "Are we supposed to sit back and do nothing?" The implicit answer to this rhetorical question—no—is the justification for the "propaganda of the deed," the heroic first stage of anarchist terror most prevalent in Russia. Russian nihilism was a fashionable cliché in contemporary literature. Perhaps one of the most interesting bad plays of the time is Oscar Wilde's first: *Vera; or, The Nihilists*, which premiered in New York on August 20, 1883. (On the poster for the premiere, the title contains a significant printing error: *Vera; or, The Nihilist*. The singular shifts the focus away from the social movement and onto the romantic, passionate individual.) The note slipped to the innocent Vera in the prologue by her brother, whom she chances to meet on his way into Siberian exile, reads: "99 Rue Tchernavaya, Moscow. To strangle whatever nature is in me; neither to love nor to be loved; neither to pity nor to be pitied; neither to marry nor to be given in marriage, till the end is come." The wording echoes *The Revolutionary Catechism* by Nechaev and Bakunin. Vera kisses the paper and says: "My brother, I shall keep the oath." After its first laconic chords, the drama takes an incredibly kitschy turn—the Tsarevitch is a member of the nihilistic secret society, and he and Vera fall in love—but at least it strikes the right note at the start: intransigency. One might describe it as the logic of nihilism before the sentimentality of the play sets in. But of course this iron logic itself is full of desperate sentimentality.

At the piano sits the sonata-playing FRIEND
While FRED *riles up the kili-kili snake,*
Then clamps it like a flower fake
In a bouquet of murderous intent.

As the Grand Duke looms up on his steed
His right cheek is grazed by the bouquet.
He dies amidst the soup course in the séparée.
The horrified Miss Lily consults the maître d'.
—RUBINER, EISENLOHR, and HAHN, "The Assassination"
(Crime Sonnets)

In the nineteenth century, terrorist acts quickly became a standard plot device in exotic penny-dreadful fiction. And this fiction, in turn, had a special affinity with a fairy-tale city which today, appallingly enough, has itself become the scene of never-ending explosions: Baghdad, the setting of the Arabian Nights, where the caliph wanders after dark in search of instructive adventures. European literature boasts a surprising number of sequels, adaptations, and pastiches of these tales, several stories by Robert Louis Stevenson being among the most remarkable. The second part of Stevenson's *New Arabian Nights* first appeared in 1885 as *The Dynamiter: More New Arabian Nights*; Stevenson wrote the stories to entertain himself during a long illness in the years 1883–1884. The first cycle had initially been published in 1878 as *Latter-Day Arabian Nights*, including what is probably the best-known of these penny-dreadful legends: "The Suicide Club," launched with a flourish by the "Story of the Young Man with the Cream Tarts." Here we meet Prince Florizel and his faithful friend Colonel Geraldine as Harun-al-Rashid and his vizier, donning urban costumes just as the caliph and his courtiers do in the Arabian tale so that they can mingle with Baghdad's crowds and probe, incognito, the life and loyalty of his subjects. ("Colonel Geraldine was dressed and painted to represent a person connected with the Press in reduced circumstances; while the Prince had, as usual, travestied his appearance by the addition of false whiskers and a pair of large adhesive eyebrows. These lent him a shaggy and weather-beaten air, which, for one of his urbanity, formed the most impenetrable disguise.") In *The Dynamiter*, Stevenson's elaborately ironic narrative strategy begins with the conflation of two mysterious cities: "In the city of encounters, the Baghdad of the West, and, to be more precise, on the broad northern pavement of Leicester Square...." London is Baghdad.

In the meantime this equation has, in its own way, entered into the history of terrorism. At one not-too-distant time, especially in America, "Baghdad" simply meant a magical place. Around 1910 one of America's great storytellers, O. Henry, called New York "old Baghdad-on-the-Subway," encapsulating the mystery of the city that endlessly produced new stories. We can see and hear what Baghdad was supposed to be in films like *Kismet* (1944, MGM, directed by William Dieterle), which absurdly and charmingly tells a Technicolor fairy tale about the good caliph, the wicked vizier, and the palace gardener. At the end the courtesan Marlene Dietrich and the thieving magician Ronald Colman, pardoned and exiled, ride out of the city into the desert; in the last shot they call out laughingly to the viewers that this is the end of a tale from "old Baghdad." "In old Baghdad"—these words are meant to evoke timeless, magical beauty, sentimental, mysterious, and innocent. Even the cities of the imagination have been ravaged.

DUMMBACH: What is this letter doing outside my door?

MARIE: It's probably from one of those Jewish lottery companies again.

DUMMBACH: Then the mailman wouldn't have tossed it on the floor of the hall, for heaven's sake. It's addressed to me. Really we ought to be a bit careful—in the newspapers you often read about letters like that exploding.

He opens the letter with outstretched hands and averted face. Is it open?

MARIE: (hiding her laughter) Not quite.

DUMMBACH: Now?

MARIE: Yes.

—ELIAS NIEBERGALL, *Datterich: Local Farce in Six Tableaus in Darmstadt Dialect* (1841)

You know something, Mr. Fielding? You're dynamite!

—JACK LEMMON to JOE E. BROWN in *Some Like It Hot*

P. G. Wodehouse's cycle of novels and stories about the appealingly foolish young Bertie Wooster and Jeeves, his valet ("gentleman's gentleman," "my man"), written between 1917 and 1974, is remarkable for its bucolic deceleration of history. In a temporal continuum in which noteworthy horse races seem to provide the narrator's main source of orientation ("She married old Tom Travers the year Bluebottle won the Cambridgeshire," or "In the autumn of the year in which Yorkshire Pudding won the Manchester November Handicap...") time's arrow seems almost suspended in midair; in *Jeeves in the Offing*, which appeared in 1960, we are reminded that Gussie Fink-Nottle had gotten roaring drunk before presenting the school prizes at Market Snodsbury "the previous summer"—a reference to the 1934 novel *Right Ho, Jeeves*. This technique entails a certain social anachronism that is simultaneously soothing and comically baffling. When Bertie Wooster tries to help his impecunious friend Bicky in New York—who has had an unexpected visit from his stingy uncle, the Duke of York, and urgently needs money— Jeeves hits on the idea of charging nobility-mad Americans five dollars for the chance to shake the hand of a duke. At first, though, it is difficult to find any takers. "By the end of a week the only name we had on our list was a delicatessen-store keeper down in Bicky's part of the town, and as he wanted us to take it out in sliced ham instead of cash that didn't help much. There was a gleam of light when the brother of Bicky's pawnbroker offered ten dollars, money down, for an introduction to old Chiswick, but the deal fell through, owing to its turning out that the chap was an anarchist and intended to kick the old boy instead of shaking hands with him. At that, it took me the deuce of a time to persuade Bicky not to grab the cash and let things take their course. He seemed to regard the pawnbroker's brother rather as a sportsman and benefactor of his species than otherwise."

(*Carry On, Jeeves!*, 1925) This is anarchism in its pastoral form, as it were, domesticated by comedy, like the socialist organization Heralds of the Red Dawn which makes a sublime appearance in *The Inimitable Jeeves*. This comedic anarchism is a figuration whose archetype lies safely in the past.

Going back a little ways, the memoirs and diaries of the Belle Époque reflect the profound disquiet of the bourgeoisie; the echoes of the anarchists' acts of terror resonate in the *Journal* of the Goncourt brothers. "This morning Pélagie came into my room and said 'What a night! A commotion on the boulevard as though a crowd of people were running to see a fire! But no, it was a troop of men and women, yelling *Vive l'anarchie!* for a whole hour.' And she gave me the morning paper, which reported the bomb explosion in Café Terminus." (February 13, 1894) The Goncourts reacted with sardonic vitriol, cursing the anarchists; but Léon Bloy, for instance, noted in his diary on June 1, 1906: "The little king of Spain"—Alfonso XIII—"on returning from the church in which he was married, was nearly torn into tiny pieces along with his queen. A bomb killed seven people and two horses, leaving him untouched. The young monarch is reported to have said the following generous words: *That is nothing.* Then he went away weeping, without a single glance at the mangled bodies." Observations of this kind do not exactly reflect sympathy for the terrorist act, but at the

THE BOMB

very least they express an intense antipathy toward its target.
A typical entry from the year 1892, preceded by an equally
typical note about Bloy's landlady, reads: "April 21. Visited
my landlady, who looks like a fat cheese set in motion by
maggots. . . . April 25. Anarchist fireworks. Powerful explosion at the wine dealer's, where Ravachol was arrested. The
virtuous people are trembling in their boots. *Spiritus ubi
vult spirat: et vocem eius audis, sed nescis unde veniat, aut quo
vadat.*" Bloy's startling citation of the Biblical phrase "The
wind bloweth where it listeth" (John 3:8) to comment on a
bomb explosion is rooted in his total rejection of the society
of "virtuous people"; he wishes the wrath of God upon them
and manages to see a volcano eruption or a fire at a charity
bazaar as a manifestation of this wrath.

In Ernst Bloch's *Traces*, amidst a series of other anecdotes,
the narrator immerses himself for a moment in the history
of anarchism. First he records an impression from everyday
life, a worker eating lobster in a working-class Parisian restaurant, an unusual sight—"Here, finally, was a good not defiled
by bourgeois enjoyment; the sweat of the deprived, the dis-
grace of capital gains didn't affect the flavor." This is followed
by another little story about the driver of a big, flashy car
who attempts to force his way through the crowds on
July 14, Bastille Day, as dancing people throng the streets,
and finds his way defiantly blocked. And thirdly: "Likewise

in Paris, a quiet man had set the following in motion two years earlier." In a café he reads in a book: "... older readers will perhaps still recall the times, and the great agitation that went through the world as the newspapers would time and again report, in very short articles, of anarchist bombings in Paris.... The bombs seemed to fly randomly into houses, into an elegant café by the St. Lazare station, into the Chamber of Deputies and into a little restaurant, even into an empty Ste. Madeleine's. A barracks was blown up, the Serbian ambassador was shot at on the street, Sadi Carnot, President of the Republic, was stabbed on the ride to the theater. It was the age of Revachol, Vaillant, Henry, Caserio, and other dangerous propagandists of the deed, the age of dynamite...." The "quiet man" immerses himself in the picturesquely menacing names of the anarchist gangs (the "Hairy Lads of Billancourt," the "Panthers of Batignolles," the "Oak Hearts of Cettes," the "Children of Nature," the "Jailbirds of Lille," the "Pillory of Sedan," the "Yatagan of Terre Noire") and learns that anarchist "newspapers ... displayed a standing rubric with the epigraph, 'Directions for the Manufacture of Nonbourgois Products.'" And when he stands up to fetch cigarettes, there is suddenly a terrible explosion. A bomb? No, he has merely knocked over a soda siphon. The alarm in the restaurant subsides, he pays for the broken bottle and gets "his cigarettes at the counter, like peace pipes"; only the young bourgeois couple at the next table is "by deep instinct not entirely satisfied with the man's merely financial penalty." Bloch ends: "If every worker ate lobster, the splinters from the seltzer bottle would hurt no feelings." That is a rather didactic conclusion, yet it precisely describes anarchism's core, the hatred of the injustice in which *nolentes volentes*, one way or the other, all the restaurant's patrons are implicated.

Close to its chronological climax, anarchism inspired one of the finest literary products from the end of the "long nineteenth century." The subtitle of the novel, published in 1908, is "A Nightmare." It is indeed one long astonishing dream of mutiny and power, loneliness and solidarity, ultimately containing something unsolvable at its center: when you try to make it out, you wake up.

G. K. Chesterton's novel *The Man Who Was Thursday* is a mystical capriccio about the great utopian dialectic of freedom and order. It is set in contemporary London, around 1900, shot through with the wistful topoi of the era's poetry: the street lamps, the organ grinders' melodies, dawn over the Thames "like the splitting of great bars of lead, showing bars of silver," the dome of St. Paul's, the feathery, ragged red evening clouds and a girl's red hair and the lanterns in a suburban garden at the beginning of the great adventure, glowing "in the dwarfish trees like some fierce and monstrous fruit." And yet it is also a curious political and philosophical meditation, unique in its interweaving of reasoning and melodramatic action. The story tells of a young man who decides, irked by the fashionable nihilistic small-talk of his day, to take up the fight against terrorism. ("He always felt that Government stood alone and desperate, with its back to the wall. He was too quixotic to have cared for it otherwise.") In a dark room, a man seen only from behind initiates him into the ranks of the anti-anarchist police. And so he is swept into an incredible whirlpool of events that upends his world view time and again; in fact, reversibility is the narrative principle, and more than once the hero feels "that all trees were growing downwards and that all stars were under his feet." He manages to work his way up to Thursday, one of the leaders of the anarchist movement, whose members are named after days of the week, and comes before the supreme President—the monstrously large, fat, unpredictable Sunday who embodies the unsolvable riddle of the adventure and the novel.

In many ways it is a brilliant penny-dreadful. The peculiar smile of Monday, the secretary, whose mouth moves only on one side of his face, appears later as a splendid *coup de théâtre*. Off in the distance the heroes detect the threatening approach of an "advancing mob," and anxiously observe them through their field glasses. The leaders of the mob are wearing black half-masks. And "presently as they talked they all smiled and one of them smiled on one side." The book abounds in moments that send a quiet thrill down the reader's spine, satisfying our insatiable desire for excitement and surprise, yet are woven into a complex speculative tale: masks and duels, terrorist acts and getaways, pursuits and conspiracies. Typically of Chesterton's work, the most powerful effects arise from the intertwining of adventure and reflection.

There is one especially powerful moment, coming as the fantastical happenings yet again become accelerated and confused, after the six days of the week have recognized each other as policemen behind the masks of nihilism: all of them have been recruited by the man in the dark room. Now they decide to confront Sunday, the monstrous, much-feared anarchist leader. As once before, the place has been chosen according to Poe's principle of conspicuous invisibility: the balcony of a restaurant overlooking Leicester Square, just big enough for an opulent champagne breakfast for seven. When asked who he really is, and why he has filled all the positions in the Anarchist Council with secret policemen, the President ("and he rose slowly to an incredible height, like some enormous wave about to arch above them and break") roars in reply that no one will ever find out. He jumps over the railing of the balcony, but before hitting the ground "like a great ball of india-rubber" and bounding off, he pulls himself up again, thrusts his gigantic round face above the railing for a moment and says: "There's one thing I'll tell you though about who I am. I am the man in the dark room, who made you all policemen."

This moment seems to crystallize the yearning of the author (a fat, ungainly man, in later life bloated to grotesque proportions) for feather-like lightness and preternatural agility, for boundless physical potential. That is one aspect. The other aspect is the paradox pronounced by Sunday: anarchy is the police, the police are anarchy. This is a fertile mystery, and it is connected with another great statement in the book, voiced by Tuesday, the most unremarkable character. At the last ceremonial meeting, the great, strange celebration held somewhere in pastoral seclusion where all the world is dancing, and Sunday listens to the questions of the days of the week (questions as to the meaning of the world), Tuesday says: "I wish I knew why I was hurt so much."

Bucolic Anti-Semitism
A Commentary

Meeting of the Cherusci's association in Krems.

> *POGATSCHNIGG, KNOWN AS TEUT: (Shouts of "Heil!" It sounds like "Hedl!")...We confidently await the moment when the wounded Muscovite bear shall slink back to its lair on bloody paws! And after him the garlic--smelling Kohn nationalists! Heil! (Shouts: Bravo! Hedl! Long live Teut! Long live Pogatschnigg!)*
>
> *A VOICE: Yidelekh! (Laughter)*
>
> —KARL KRAUS, *The Last Days of Mankind*, Act 3, Scene 11

FROM A PURELY abstract perspective, the exploration of the history of anti-Semitism—given the utterly bizarre and hence fascinating character of this elaborate delusional system and its countless auxiliary mythologies—could be just as entertaining as the structurally comparable lunatic fringes of cultural history: UFOs, the true author of Shakespeare's works, the pyramid prophecies. But the pages of these pamphlets and books are shadowed by a vast horror, and you realize that though this, too, is a speculative muddle, it arises from inconceivable malice. It is impossible not to feel the chill of barbarism; yet for a few moments particularly outré effusions of madness inspire a covert desire to laugh. This laughter literally sticks in your throat when reading mind-boggling statements such as "For this reason, it is not advisable to deport the Jews to Siberia; given their climatic toughness, that would only stimulate their health still further." (Hitler's Table Talk, May 29, 1942)

When you delve into the prehistory of the genocide, into this rhizome of blithe hatred, fantasy, and obsessive attempts to explain the world, you eventually arrive at a peculiar point. Leafing through the brochures and pamphlets from the nationalist *Vereine* (clubs, associations), you find the political existing side by side with a jolly conviviality—and a key element of this jolliness is the defamation and humiliation of the "Other." It is a textbook confirmation of the insight that the personal is political. Aggressive rejection of the Jews—supposedly usurious and lecherous, guilty of treachery and subversion—is bad enough, but a still deeper pathology is indicated when one's club activities or vacationing enjoyment is not emotionally complete if no defamation of the Jews is involved. Here anti-Semitism has a penchant for centering on an element of mirth, of cheerful smugness. One of its strategies is the mocking song, which, like anonymous letters, venomous advertisements in nationalist newspapers, runic embellishments and lectures on the Edda, the blood to be kept pure, and the dagger plunged into the back of the German army, lends relish to the ritual of self-affirmation.

These anti-Semitic songs are mostly forgotten today, apart from the borderline case of the rhyme "Haben Sie nicht den kleinen Kohn gesehen?" ("Haven't You Seen Little Cohn?") first sung by Guido Thielscher in the play *Seine Kleine* at Berlin's Thalia-Theater, which operates only indirectly with an anti-Semitic topos. But historical scholarship has preserved them. We can hear the echoes of the song which the spa guests on a certain North Sea island sang each evening from the 1880s to the time of the Weimar Republic:

We greet you in our gladsome song, O lovely Borkum strand.
Where through the air the seagull glides, and green is all the land!
Where the wild sea of northern climes bedews the dunes with spray,
Where the lighthouse beam, from its proud height, shows mariners the way.
Thus we loudly sing your praise, we guests from near and far,

Let the ardent cry ring out: Borkum hurrah! Borkum
    hurrah!

There may be many splendid spas all through our
    fatherland,
But none as dear to us as you, you splendorous island
    strand,
Under your enchantment how cares do seem to fade!
How fresh and light the heart becomes, how cheerful
    grows the gaze!
Thus we loudly sing your praise, we guests from near
    and far,
Let the ardent cry ring out: Borkum hurrah! Borkum
    hurrah!

In this green island land there's a German spirit true.
And so all those of our own tribe come joyfully to you.
Germanity reigns on Borkum's strand, and Germany's
    banner waves.
The purity of Germania's shield we shall forever save!
But whoe'er flat-footed, hook-nosed and dark-curled
    slinks along
He must not enjoy your strand, he must begone, he
    must begone!
Begone!

The guests would hardly have gathered every evening to belt out this song in chorus if it had only sung the clumsy praise of natural beauty or the purity of Germania's shield. No, the emotional justification of the entire song comes with the last lines; the real treat is to be with like-minded people singing lustily of the hooked noses and flat feet of those who are not tolerated on Borkum. The cathartic repetition of "Begone!" in the very last line enacts the utopia of the anti-Semite—the expulsion of the Jews, their obliteration from one's environment. The landmark study by Frank Bajohr, *Unser Hotel ist judenfrei: Bäder-Antisemitismus im 19. und 20. Jahrhundert* (Our Hotel is Jew Free: Anti-Semitism in 19th and 20th Century Spas) with its appendix of hate songs ("O Wangeroog, how low you have sunk / Your shore was always so free from Jewish rabble. ...") takes one detail, minor but representative in its imperishable filth, to document the extent to which the convivial social life of the German bourgeoisie and petty bourgeoisie around 1900 was permeated by the aggressively celebrated ostracism of the (real and imaginary) Jews.

The Borkum song circulated on postcards as well. Joke postcards, which to this day offer a fallback option in resort town souvenir shops, tended in other countries to be on the apolitical side. In an illuminating essay ("The Art of Donald McGill," 1942) on the winkingly obscene comic postcards found at English bathing resorts, George Orwell explicitly emphasized this aspect. Leafing through collections, one finds at most the occasional little joke (not necessarily unfunny) such as the 1935 cartoon of a frazzled traveling salesman saying: "I'm telling you—if Hitler wants any more territory, he can have mine!" In contrast, German postcard humor has a marked patriotic and political bent, usually expressed in xenophobic terms. There is an astonishingly high proportion of anti-Semitic images and slogans on German-language postcards from various spa towns (Bad Kissingen, Karlsbad, Franzensbad, etc.), on postcards sold by individual hotels and restaurants (such as the Kölnischer Hof, "Frankfurt's only Jew-free hotel"), and on postcards for general use with pre-printed "Greetings from—" An especially common motif is that of ejection (of a Jewish guest from a "German restaurant," or the entire Jewish population from Germany). Again and again, the primitive rhymes revolve around one thing: Begone! One of the most infamous pieces of anti-Semitic literature is Elvira Bauer's Nazi children's book *Trau keinem Fuchs auf grüner Heid und keinem Jud bei seinem Eid* (Never Trust a Fox on the Green Heath, nor the Oath of a Jew, probably 1937). In the final image, which shows the Jews leaving the country—as always, they are depicted as grotesque and repellent figures—a blond boy with the traditional pointed cap denoting the plain honest German enthusiastically plays the concertina; the signpost says in old German script: "One way / hurry, hurry / The Jews are our misfortune!"

The swiftest horseman, that is Death,
With a juppheidi and a juppheida,
The flag waves proudly black-white-red.
Hurrah, Germania!
—KLABUND, "German Folk Song"

Find your peace where songs are gaily ringing!
Evil people never cared for singing.
—Folk version of JOHANN GOTTFRIED SEUME's "Songs"
(1804)

Sung ridicule, usually formulaic, is widespread, and was still more widespread in earlier times. Mocking songs probably make up a significant part of the repertoire of genuine folk-songs. Here we find ridicule of professions or regions ("The Tyroleans are merry...," "My father is an Appenzeller..."). It is difficult to say whether these songs were sung in a confrontational context; there is some evidence to that effect, for instance of songs that are sung when someone leaves the pub early and his companions suspect he has run out of money: "And then Jörgli and his comrades sang the teasing song, pounding their fists on the table," as Berthold Auerbach writes in "Der Tolpatsch" (The Blunderhead, 1842). There was something that could be described as vocational mockery, targeting pretty much most professions, though an especially striking example was the satiric depiction of tailors. Folk culture regularly portrays tailors as figures of fun: scrawny, sickly, fearful, the very embodiment of cowardice. There is a surprisingly large number of folksongs ridiculing tailors: "And when the tailors had their holiday, they all were filled with glee; / Ninety, yea nine times ninety-nine dined on one roast flea...," or the "Tailor's Wedding": "A stuffed goat's hide, that's the tailor's bride...," etc. The tailor is skinny and weak (even as a demonic figure in *Struwwelpeter*, where he rushes through the door "with the big, sharp scissors" as the thumb-sucker's quasi-castrator, he is extremely thin—otherwise he would not be recognizable as a tailor). In the work of Wilhelm Busch, in certain respects a latter-day compendium of folk themes, we encounter the tailor not only as the automatic butt of teasing in *Max and Moritz* (with the typical goat jokes: "Tailor, tailor, meh, meh, meh!"), but also in smaller works for *Fliegende Blätter* such as "Die Ballade von den sieben Schneidern" (The Ballad of the Seven Tailors) or "Romanze" (Romance): "The tailor cried: 'Faithless woman—to be so misled! / Had I ne'er known you at all!' / He went and bought a piece of thread / And hanged himself from the wall." The suicide technique illustrates the desperate man's scant weight: a piece of thread is enough to hold him.

A typical example for ridiculing despised professions appears in passing in the first act of *The Weavers*, by Gerhart Hauptmann, which contrasts the misery of the cottage workers delivering their goods with the smug affluence of the factory owner's office. Here it is the clerks who excel at the contemptuous treatment of the workers, who cower like suppliants. When one of the desperate women, begging for a tiny advance, blurts out: "We've a lot o' little ones...," the cashier and the apprentice look at each other in amusement. "Neumann *half aside to the Apprentice, in a serio-comic tone*: 'Every year brings a child to the linen-weaver's wife, heigh-ho, heigh-ho, heigh.' Apprentice *takes up the rhyme, half singing*: 'And the little brat it's blind the first weeks of its life, heigh-ho, heigh-ho, heigh.'"

This sort of folk mockery, also manifested in the teasing that takes place between the inhabitants of certain cities or towns, can be seen as a parallel form to early anti-Semitism, but there is a huge difference to be taken into account. This invective still belongs somehow to what Joseph Conrad once called "the tempest of good-humored and meaningless curses" (*The Nigger of the "Narcissus,"* 1897), a ritualized form of communication free from strong *ad hominem* aggression. This ridicule—like the tradition of the "prank" with its slightly sadistic tinge, numerous variations of which, up until a generation or two ago, were found in most books for young people—forms something of a basis, a breeding ground for modern persecutory ridicule, but the latter is no longer content to enact the playful ritual of a stratified society or the ambivalent anarchy of childhood; it seeks to wound and humiliate vulnerable outsiders. A typical feature of the context we are exploring here is the fusion of this malice with the rituals of German *Verein* and vacation activities.

What drove them? What guided them? Even today, thirty-five years later, as I reflect on this past with mature, cool rationality, it seems to me that I still lack certain elements for a solution to this question.
—LÉON BLUM on the anti-Dreyfusards, *L'affaire Dreyfus,* 1935

There are occasional descriptions of the *Verein* from the period around 1900, mainly as a place of intrigue (as in Josef Ruedinger's *Die Fahnenweihe* [The Consecration of the Flag], 1895). Nineteenth-century German *Vereine* are a phenomenon deserving of extensive investigation; satiric depictions from the time, mostly in a mild vein, focus on the diligent zeal devoted to the pursuit of *Gemütlichkeit*. This in itself is a force to be reckoned with. Few German words have had so ill-starred a career as *"gemütlich."* David Hansemann's proverbial phrase "There's an end to *Gemütlichkeit* as soon as it comes to money"—already clearly reflecting the jocose, tongue-in-cheek transformation of a word stemming from the sphere of Romantically introspective *"Gemüt"* (roughly "soul")—was coined in 1847 at the Prussian Parliament, and followed in 1850 by a song praising the *Stammtisch*, or pub gathering, "Die Ritter von der Gemütlichkeit" (The Knights of *Gemütlichkeit*). In the era of Wagner's *Ring*, where Wotan in *Siegfried* bursts out in "joyfully *gemütliches* laughter," we have already advanced quite far into a phase in which *"Gemütlichkeit,"* in architecture, social life, and German self-understanding, becomes a program of defensive pride; fused with the tone of barked-out commands, it forms the timbre we hear in the Kaiser's words at an 1889 reception in Strasbourg: "... and in every way the city makes me feel at home." Here *Gemütlichkeit* has become something like a mask of self-appreciative power.

The documentation accompanying Tankred Dorst's *Rotmord oder I Was a German* (Red Murder or I Was a German, 1969, TV drama based on Dorst's 1968 play *Toller*), compiled by Dorst, Peter Zadek, and Hartmut Gehrke, includes the lyrics and score of a nationalist song for a solo voice and chorus that addresses the representatives of Munich's Soviet Republic using motifs from the most vulgar repertoire of anti-Semitism ("O Moses! O Moses! Look at those crooked noses!). "And that little Mühsam cries: Everywhere you see our guys! / And that little Toller-Cohn / is eyeing the Messiah's throne!" This is accompanied by an imitation of the supposedly typical gestures ("Talking, talking with his hands, / He runs up so fast he pants"). The elaborate staging of the sort of ad hoc song whose natural habitat is the *Verein* evening evokes the pleasures of people who feel particularly cozy when their social *Gemütlichkeit* depends on vilifying others.

Construing turn-of-the-century German anti-Semitism as a type of pathology, one could take the approach often used in medicine and law and study several classic cases that display crucial traits with great vividness. For anyone wishing to explore this terrain, three publications especially recommend themselves; though different in form and style, they are linked by their manic collector's zeal, their intransigence, their denunciatory vein, and their sheer lunacy. All these works appeared after World War I, but vividly reflect the accumulation and crystallization of fantasies reaching far back into the nineteenth century: the encyclopedia

Sigilla veri, the genealogical work *Semi-Gotha,* and the polemics of Mathilde Ludendorff. These works, testimonials to a toxic monomania, are distorting mirrors, but—if the oxymoron is permissible—they are highly precise ones.

The *Sigilla veri* was published in several volumes beginning in 1929. The subtitle of this book was: "(Ph. Stauff's Semi-Kürschner). Encyclopedia of the Jews and Their Allies and Adversaries of All Times and Regions, Germany in Particular, the Doctrines, Customs, Stratagems and Statistics of the Jews along with Their Argot, Pseudonyms, Secret Societies, etc.... Edited by E. Ekkehard." Philip Stauff (1876–1923) was a central figure in the spheres of *völkisch,* esoteric anti-Semitism, especially Guido "von" List's Ariosophy; "E. Ekkehard" is probably Heinrich Kraeger. This infinitely flabbergasting work, whose title promises the insignia or imprimatur of the truth, is probably the only lengthy reference work in existence that is based entirely on the principle of paranoia. It was never completed, but its four volumes and several fascicles did get as far as the entry for "Rathenau." Envy, direct denunciation (the addresses of the Jewish dentists in a random small town), sexual phobia—"Sexual intercourse between Germanic people and Jews (see: blonde women)," hatred of modernity, conspiracy fantasies—all this is disgorged in a tone that continually fluctuates between the pathos of the Teutonic apocalypse and the stolid jollity of the man of the world who likes to tell jokes and knows a "secret" Jewish punch line for every situation in the world. At the same time, the character of the entire work is extremely private, yet with far-reaching social ramifications—behind it one detects a tireless federation of envious lunatics working together in solidarity. As a *pars pro toto*, in the entry on "Stefan George" (described here as a Jew), we read: "A friend writes us: 'Going by the portrait, I didn't think St. G. looks Jewish. Until it occurred to me that a Russian Jew of my acquaintance has a similar type of face.'"

The *Semi-Gotha* ("Weimar Historic-Genealogical Vade-Mecum of All the Nobility of Yehudean Origin. List of All Those with Jewish Blood in the Male Line...etc.," 1912) and its various follow-up works are devoted to proving the "Judaization" of the German aristocracy, listing real or alleged genealogical details along the lines of the *Almanach de Gotha*. The culmination of the anonymous work, written by Wilhelm Pickl v. Witkenberg (1866–1922), was the volume *Semi-Imperator*, which claimed to prove that Wilhelm II and the Hohenzollern family had Jewish blood (naturally a conclusive explanation for the downfall of the German Reich). In both cases—*Semi-Kürschner, Semi-Gotha*—the "Semi-" is an abbreviation for "Semites," though the meaning "half" still resonates. Pickl's works, too, are an idiosyncratic amalgam of unreliable information and pure invective, anecdotal digressions and pseudo-scientific sermons. I will now take a closer look at Mathilde Ludendorff, because mockery plays such a major role in her most important work; mockingness is described as a fundamental trait of the Jews even as this fantasy is mirrored by the author.

When the German *Kaiserreich* lost World War I and the Kaiser fled ignominiously to Holland, the hour of conspiracy fantasies had come, centering on the stab-in-the-back legend: that the German army, "unvanquished in the field," could only have been defeated due to treason on the home front. All the resentments of the German petty bourgeoisie now merged in an obsession painstakingly cultivated by the radical right: Germany was the victim of secret foes, the socialists, the Jesuits, the Freemasons, the Jews. In 1928 this anti-Semitic mania produced a work with the dramatic title *Der ungesühnte Frevel an Lessing, Luther, Mozart und Schiller. Ein Betrag zur Deutschen Kulturgeschichte* (The Unatoned Sacrilege against Lessing, Luther, Mozart and Schiller: A Contribution to German Cultural History), which was followed by various expanded editions and reprints.

The author was Dr. Mathilde Ludendorff, née von Kemnitz, who came to prominence through her third husband, Erich von Ludendorff, Germany's most famous World War I military leader next to Hindenburg. Toward the end of the war, the military reversal plunged him into a profound psychological crisis; now, in the 1920s, he developed a system of paranoid delusion aimed at absolving him of guilt in Germany's defeat. Under his wife's influence, he spiraled deeper and deeper into a compulsively anti-Semitic ideology that dragged a comet's tail of lunatic publications through the twenties and the thirties. The more glowingly the Ludendorffs depicted the essence of German ethnicity in their writings (their journal was entitled *Am heiligen Quell deutscher Kraft*, At the Sacred Fount of German Strength), the more incomprehensible was the nation's ongoing streak of bad luck—it became comprehensible only when one held the key to the diabolical machinations aimed against the Germans. For apparently Luther, Lessing, Mozart, and Schiller—and many other great men such as Fichte, Leibniz, Nietzsche, Schubert, Bach, and Haydn—had been murdered by agents of a Jewish-Freemason conspiracy as part of an all-encompassing plan to rob the German people of their creative spiritual powers. Mathilde Ludendorff, who tried to prove that all the victims had been systematically mocked and humiliated as well, made Mozart's funeral into a "criminal's burial in a mass grave," describing the whole episode as "The lodge's murder of Mozart and the curse on his remains." The following section, "The 'Invisible Fathers' Revenge upon Schiller and His Death 'At the Right Time'" is the book's centerpiece. Here it launches a frontal attack on the liberal, humanistic "spirit of Weimar."

In Mathilde Ludendorff's fevered imagination, Schiller was poisoned in Weimar by a camarilla of Masonic doctors and false friends due to his attempt to disengage himself from the Freemasons and his increasingly harsh condemnation of the French Revolution. And the strange fate of his corpse and his skull reflected a Jewish curse upon the outcast. "The city of Weimar," wrote Mathilde Ludendorff, "is defiled among Germany's cities for all time because it allowed Jewish vengeance to run riot unhindered ... with Schiller's remains." This political agitation grew louder and louder until at last in 1936 the Goethe Society spoke out severely against Ludendorff's travesty, and its president Julius Petersen declared that if these sorts of accounts gained currency, "all classical Weimar ... would appear as a den of criminals, and the German people, having let its greatest men, from Luther onward, come to their deaths in this way, would seem a band of murderers." In the end, with a bad grace, the Nazi propaganda ministry put out a press release: "Speculations on Schiller's death are prohibited." Mathilde Ludendorff, who had indeed referred to Weimar as "the Masonic Duke Karl August von Weimar's hotbed of criminals," always reserved her profoundest contempt for Goethe.

One of the most interesting aspects of this delusive conspiracy theory is the extent to which its author's own most lunatic traits are projected onto "the Jews." Ludendorff searched obsessively for days and years of particular numerological significance (especially conducive to murders) on the theory that the Jews, with their dark superstitions, were notorious for choosing such "Yahweh days" to commit crucial crimes. And these imaginary Jewish crimes were marked by an obsessive desire to mock enemies even in death. "The stubborn superstition of the malevolent Jews, which discharged itself in such dreadful fashion upon the creators of our people's culture," entails something like a magical obligation to mock without ceasing. Yet in truth this curse rests on the shoulders of Mathilde Ludendorff and the anti-Semites, all of whose utterances are pervaded by their own permanent, reflexive mockery of a Jewry imagined as ugly and ludicrous in all its manifestations. While fanning the fear of the "Jew who hates and mocks our blood," this same Jew must constantly be insulted; it is as though they cannot stop making faces at him. In the traits fantastically ascribed to Jewry, the anti-Semite projects a description of herself and her kind, not least—yearningly—in the trait of global power. What a mirror image! From a structural perspective—to return to my starting point—this process would be superbly comical, were it not stained by so much unmetaphorical blood.

Translator's Note

In *Gaslight* Joachim Kalka quotes from many writers in many languages, and in translating the book from German I have relied on the work of other translators, credited below. Any translation not otherwise credited is my own.
—I. F. C.

Theodor W. Adorno, *Alban Berg: Master of the Smallest Link*, translated by Juliane Brand and Christopher Hailey. Céleste Albaret, *Monsieur Proust*, translated by Barbara Bray. Honoré de Balzac, *The Ball at Sceaux*, translated by Clara Bell. Honoré de Balzac, *Father Goriot*, translated by Ellen Marriage. Honoré de Balzac, *Letters to Madame Hanska, born Countess Rzewuska, afterwards Madame Honoré de Balzac, 1833–1846*, translated by Katharine Prescott Wormeley. Honoré de Balzac, *Rise and Fall of César Birotteau*, translated by Katharine Prescott Wormeley. Honoré de Balzac, *A Woman of Thirty*, translated by Ellen Marriage. Walter Benjamin, *One-Way Street and Other Writings*, translated by Edmund Jephcott and Kingsley Shorter. Ernst Bloch, *Traces*, translated by Anthony A. Nassar. Bertolt Brecht, *The Threepenny Opera*, translated by Ralph Manheim and John Willet. Fyodor Dostoevsky, *Demons: A Novel in Three Parts*, translated by Richard Pevear and Larissa Volokhonsky. Fyodor Dostoevsky, *The Notebooks for "The Possessed,"* translated by Victor Terras, edited by Edward Wasiolek. Friedrich Engels to

Margaret Harkness, April 1888, e-publication, https://www.marxists. org/archive/marx/works/1888/letters/88_04_15.htm. Gustave Flaubert, *Early Writings*, translated by Robert Griffin. Gustave Flaubert, *Madame Bovary*, translated by Eleanor Marx-Aveling. Gustave Flaubert, *November: Fragments in a Nondescript Style*, translated by Andrew Brown. Theodor Fontane, "The Bridge by the Tay," in *A Harvest of German Verse*, translated and edited by Margarete Münsterberg. Johann Wolfgang von Goethe, *Conversations of Goethe with Eckermann and Soret*, translated by John Oxenford. Johann Wolfgang von Goethe, *Maxims and Reflections*, translated by Elisabeth Stopp, edited by Peter Hutchison. Johann Wolfgang von Goethe, *Miscellaneous Travels of J. W. Goethe*, edited by L. Dora Schmitz. Gerhart Hauptmann, *The Dramatic Works of Gerhart Hauptmann*, translated and edited by Ludwig Lewisohn. Theodor Herzl, *The Complete Diaries of Theodor Herzl*, vol. 1, edited by Raphael Patai, translated by Harry Zohn. Franz Kafka, "A Country Doctor," translated by Willa and Edwin Muir. Franz Kafka, *Diaries, 1910–1923*, translated by Joseph Kresh, Martin Greenberg, and Hannah Arendt. Franz Kafka, *The Metamorphosis*, translated by Susan Bernofsky, edited by Mark M. Anderson. Franz Kafka, *The Trial*, translated by Breon Mitchell. Count Harry Kessler, *Journey to the Abyss: The Diaries of Count Harry Kessler, 1880–1918*, translated and edited by Laird M. Easton. Søren Kierkegaard, *Kierkegaard's Writings, XXIII: "The Moment" and Late Writings*, translated and edited by Howard V. Hong and Edna H. Hong. Karl Kraus, *The Last Days of Mankind: A Tragedy in Five Acts*, translated by Patrick Healy. Leonardo da Vinci, *The Notebooks of Leonardo Da Vinci*, translated by R. C. Bell and Edward John Poynter, edited by Jean Paul Richter, eBook, http://www.sacred-texts. com/aor/dv/index.htm. Petronius, *The Satyricon*, translated by William Arrowsmith. Marcel Proust, *In Search of Lost Time*, translated by C. K. Scott Moncrieff and Terence Kilmartin, revised by D. J. Enright. Rainer Maria Rilke, *Sonnets to Orpheus*, translated by Stephen Mitchell. Duc de Saint-Simon, *The Memoirs of Louis XIV*, vol. 1, translated by Bayle St. John. Friedrich Schiller, *The Ghost-Seer; or Apparitionist*, and *The*

TRANSLATOR'S NOTE

Sport of Destiny, in *Complete Works of Friedrich Schiller, Volume 3*. Friedrich Schiller, *The Robbers: A Tragedy*, in *The Works of Frederick Schiller: Early Dramas and Romances*, translated and edited by Henry G. Bohn. Fritz Strich, *Goethe and World Literature*, translated by C. A. M. Sym. Snorri Sturluson, "Gylfaginning," in *The Younger Edda*, translated by Rasmus Björn Anderson. Jacques Tardi, *The Arctic Marauder*, translated by Kim Thompson. Ivan Sergeevich Turgenev, *Fathers and Sons*, translated by Eugene Schuyler. Alfred de Vigny, *Servitude and Grandeur of Arms*, translated by Roger Gard. Richard Wagner, *Götterdämmerung*, translated by Frederick Jameson. Richard Wagner, *Opera and Drama*, translated by William Ashton Ellis. Richard Wagner, *The Valkyrie*, translated by Frederick Jameson.

JOACHIM KALKA is an essayist, literary critic, and translator of authors such as Martin Amis, Angela Carter, G. K. Chesterton, Nathaniel Hawthorne, Christopher Isherwood, and Gilbert Sorrentino. He lives in Leipzig, Germany.

ISABEL FARGO COLE is a writer and a translator of such authors as Annemarie Schwarzenbach, Franz Fühmann, Wolfgang Hilbig, and Klaus Hoffer. She lives in Berlin, Germany.